Rave Reviews for *The Stepmom's Book of Boundaries*

Whether stepmoms **(S)**, moms **(M)** or a combination of both **(S/M)**, women who fill a variety of personal and professional roles are raving about the advice and insights you'll find in *The Stepmom's Book of Boundaries: How and Where to Draw the Line—for a Happier, Healthier Stepfamily* by Claudette Chenevert.

"*The Stepmom's Book of Boundaries* is a must-read for moms with 'blended' families and is the seminal key to successful stepparenting. Author Claudette Chenevert reveals the secret to creating a happy life with 'yours, mine, ours' while respecting the marriage, the family unit and the individuals within. She addresses the tough stuff we all encounter, teaching us to confront it head-on." – Patti Cotton, CEO & President of Cotton Group, LLC **(S/M)**

"Being a stepmom is a sensitive balancing act. Only those who've been there truly understand the curve balls stepfamily life throws our way, making *The Stepmom's Book of Boundaries* a must-read for anyone with young or adult stepchildren. Claudette's warm tone draws us in and her advice proves that she speaks from experience—knowing that not all stepmoms deal with the same situations. Appropriate boundaries are necessary for healthy relationships of all types. I look forward to implementing Claudette's suggestions within our family and, as a result, anticipate a healthier dynamic." – Brenda Durr, Asst. Retail Manager **(S)**

"Claudette tackles a difficult topic which is essential for effective parenting but hard to truly understand, much less act on. With *The Stepmom's Book of Boundaries*, she fosters a new understanding of exactly what boundaries are, how they shape family life and how stepmoms can apply them. Claudette directly addresses issues no one wants to tackle, including how accepting responsibility leads to improved relationships. Hers is an honest, straight-forward and truly useful guide that can benefit any parent." – Sandy Fowler, Speaker, Coach & "Mighty Parenting" Co-Host **(M)**

"While *The Stepmom's Book of Boundaries* is essential for new stepparents, it reminds all of us that retrospection and retooling are critical to healthy stepfamily relationships. The way Claudette defines boundaries and expectations sang to me. By covering topics from cell phone use to sexual boundaries, as well, she provides a guide for developing trust. That alone makes it well worth reading." – Lesley Kordella, Biologist **(S)**

"Thank you for this outstanding guide, Claudette! I loved reading *The Stepmom's Book of Boundaries* and wish I had access to such insight and guidance when I began raising my two stepchildren almost 40 years ago. All four of my children would have benefited and I would have benefited, too, by having much better relationships with them. The help you bring to stepmoms through your stepfamily coaching service and now this book is amazing. Stepmoms across the world—and their partners—are sure to benefit from it. I hope stepdads also pick up a copy!" – Josy Labbe, Elder & Students Commission of Canada "Unite & Ignite" Campaign Coordinator **(S/M)**

"Just as businesses and organizations need structure and guidelines to operate effectively, so do families. Yet, stepmoms may find it difficult to talk about boundaries without stepping on toes. Claudette Chenevert makes navigating that topic easier, by outlining ways to initiate thoughtful conversations with our partners and to gain confidence in our boundary-setting capabilities. The must-have advice she shares, in *The Stepmom's Book of Boundaries*, applies to family dynamics of all kinds—if what you ultimately want is a thriving and happy household." – Meg Martines, City of South Euclid Community Center Director **(S)**

"*The Stepmom's Book of Boundaries* is long overdue and will help so many build healthy boundaries for healthy relationships. I love how Claudette describes what boundaries are, what they aren't and why we need them. Stepfamilies everywhere will benefit from her expertise and guidance. I wish this book was available when I first became a stepmom!" – Peggy Nolan, Owner of Twisted Crochet & Yoga Instructor **(S/M)**

"I wish I had a copy of *The Stepmom's Book of Boundaries* when I first became a stepmom. Fifteen years later, I'm privy to a slew of related products. Still, it's difficult to find resources for stepmoms which are as targeted, focused and plainly-written as this one. Claudette Chenevert engages couples with warmth and humor, sharing stories and anecdotes which bring her advice to life. Her book is designed to help you and your partner navigate stepfamily realities. Thank your lucky stars you found it!" – Brenda Ockun, Founder & Publisher of *StepMom Magazine* **(S)**

"What Claudette has done in *The Stepmom's Book of Boundaries* is amazing: She shares her stepmom experience in such relatable, empathic terms. The act of setting boundaries is difficult for us all. For stepmoms, it can be even more daunting. Not only does Claudette give stepmoms permission to set healthy boundaries; she lays out simple steps for doing that. I highly recommend this book for stepmoms and those who love them." – Mercedes Samudio, LCSW, Parenting Coach & Best-Selling Author of *Shame-Proof Parenting*

"Boundaries are one of the most important elements in creating a home you'd like to live in. So, whether you're a stepmom or otherwise in a 'blended' family, this book is a *must*. Claudette shares the ins-and-outs of setting boundaries, explains how they function and outlines the many choices you have. This book will not disappoint!" – Lisa Teal-Webb (aka Buckeye Bonusmom), Stepmom Peer Support Specialist **(S)**

"Being a stepmother comes with many challenges—from feeling like an outsider in your own home to dealing with difficult ex-spouses. In *The Stepmom's Book of Boundaries*, Claudette Chenevert provides practical advice that will help you set boundaries and take the brave actions needed to meet your challenges with greater clarity, confidence, compassion and courage." – Margie Warrell, Best-Selling Author of *Find Your Courage* and *Brave* **(M)**

THE
STEPMOM'S
BOOK OF
BOUNDARIES

THE STEPMOM'S BOOK OF BOUNDARIES

How and Where to Draw the Line—for a Happier, Healthier Stepfamily

Claudette Chenevert

Claudette Chenevert
Marshall, VA 20115
Https://StepmomCoach.com

Limits of Liability and Disclaimer of Warranty
The author and publisher shall not be liable for your misuse of this material.
This book is strictly for informational and educational purposes.

Warning – Disclaimer
The purpose of this book is to educate and inform. The author and/or publisher do not guarantee that anyone following these techniques, suggestions, tips, ideas, or strategies will become successful. The author and/or publisher shall have neither liability nor responsibility to anyone with respect to any loss or damage caused, or alleged to be caused, directly or indirectly by the information contained in this book.

Editor: Christine G. Adamo
Cover Design: Christine G. Adamo
Author Head Shot: Claudette Chenevert
"Brady Myth" Cover Art: Christine G. Adamo
"Brady Myth" images sourced at OnePixel and photographed by:

    Top (l. to r.): Giulio Fornasar, Tierneymj, Josep Suria
    Middle (l. to r.): Odua Images, Gpoint Studio, Andy Dean Photography
    Bottom (l. to r.): Gpoint Studio, Rido, Amazingmikael

The Stepmom's Book of Boundaries
How and Where to Draw the Line—for a Happier, Healthier Stepfamily
by Claudette Chenevert

Print ISBN-13: 978-1-7336465-1-2
Ebook ISBN-13: 978-1-7336465-0-5
Printed in the United States of America
Library of Congress Control Number: 2019901126

*To my son ... and to my
stepdaughters. Thank you for helping us
create healthy boundaries in our own family.
And to my husband, Bernard, who always
lets me test the boundaries—but is
smart enough to know
when enough is
enough!*

CONTENTS

FOREWORD

B oy, what I would've given to have my own copy of *The Stepmom's Book of Boundaries* when I first became a stepmom. While I can hardly believe it myself, that was nearly 15 years ago. Though there are times in stepfamily life when it feels as if nothing happens fast enough, one day you turn around and—poof! Your stepkids are no longer toddlers who are singing along with a cartoon aardvark to the opening theme of *Arthur*. Or, maybe they are, but now it's while they're busy packing up their rooms in preparation for their freshman years at college.

As the founder and publisher of *StepMom Magazine*, a monthly online magazine specializing in topics which matter primarily to stepmoms, over the years I've been privy to and had behind-the-scenes access to a wide range of related products. That includes books in print and books in-progress. Outside of a number of significant academic studies and research projects conducted and spearheaded by stepfamily professionals (whose own ties to stepfamily life often run quite deep and may even span generations) I know, firsthand, that it's still pretty difficult for the everyday stepmom to find resources which are as targeted, focused on their concerns and plainly-written as this one.

Its author, Claudette Chenevert, has been a *StepMom* contributor for some time. Because of this, I also know how seriously she takes: her commitment to relationship repair work, her stepmom coaching practice and her desire to share the hard-won knowledge she's gained (as a mom and a stepmom) with women like her and the partners they love. On top of that, I can always count on Claudette to tell it like it is while incorporating hefty doses of warmth and humor into her writing. I also know that she'd never shy away from sharing a difficult personal story or amusing anecdote that would help bring her advice to life and is aimed at saving the rest of us—and the families we and our partners have chosen to create for ourselves, in spite of the inherent pitfalls—a whole lot of unnecessary hoo-ha.

1

The Stepmom's Book of Boundaries is a perfect example of that. Can you research boundaries, House Rules and consequences on your own? I have no doubt! Have I made sure to cover those topics in my own publication? Yes. More than once, in fact. Could you and your partner simply call a Stepfamily Meeting and have it run relatively smoothly without any kind of outside help? It's possible, but it could still go south pretty quickly. What stepmoms like you and I want, crave and, at times, desperately need is another stepmom by our sides. Someone who's willing to do the work and dig into the facts or figures, bringing it all together in a single, stunning package which reminds us that no matter *how* complicated stepfamily life can be, we're never alone.

Every single day—scratch that, nearly every single hour of every day—I hear from stepmoms around the globe who are feeling fragile, close to broken and ready to give it all up. They sometimes feel like strangers in their own homes. They may even feel rejected by the very people they're trying so hard to please (most of them pint-sized or teenaged). At their lowest points, these women can even feel sorely misunderstood or maligned by their partners. Vows of "for better or worse" echo through their brains, as they struggle to make sense of the complications that naturally come from trying to merge two families. Or assimilate into a family system that was damaged long before they came on the scene, though at every turn they're made painfully aware that they could've simply opted out.

I say "they." Scratch that! What I really mean is: *we*. We stepmoms of society are hard-pressed to get a fair shake. The ex may hate us. The kids may hate us. Disney films repeatedly make an evil and sometimes wicked mockery of us and our relationship status. Each of us is as unique as our own stepfamily situations are, yet we have so many things in common that we swear we were destined to commiserate over, of all things, shared heartache. We've all been told, "You knew what you were getting into!" Not just by strangers, mind you. Family members and close friends can be quick to jump on that bandwagon, too: "Thanks for the news flash," we wanna say, "but you have *no* idea."

Nothing in life ever goes as planned. We *all* know that by now. But, if you plan ahead to meet the challenges stepfamily life is sure to present you with—and, believe me, there'll be no shortage of those—you'll be positioned to ride out that roller coaster with your head held high and your dignity intact. One day, you may even get the courage to let go of that bar and wave your hands in the air. True, you won't always be amused by the company you're forced to keep or the detours you're forced to take along the way. However, kicking and screaming won't do anyone any good; least of all you. You deserve to be able to look back on your relationship and your participation in raising your partner's kids as one wild ride that, in the end, was worth the price of admission.

Think of *The Stepmom's Book of Boundaries*, by Claudette Chenevert, as the theme park map that'll help you find your way out of the maze that's become your day-to-day reality. And thank your lucky stars you found it!

Fondly,
Brenda

Brenda Ockun
Founder & Publisher, *StepMom Magazine*
Publisher@StepMomMagazine.com

PREFACE

D o you feel as if your rights are being trampled on? As if, when it comes to some of the most significant relationships in your life, your desires continually go unheard by others? Do you wish everyone in your stepfamily home could benefit from healthier, happier and more peaceful interactions? If so, I bet you also wonder how you can turn what sometimes feels like a battleground into a safe haven for you and for those you care about most.

What you need, dear stepmom, are boundaries. I speak from nearly three decades of experience, knowing full well how a lack of boundaries can incite conflict, confusion and anxiety. An absence of boundaries in the home can also lead to dangerous imbalances in power. Healthy boundaries do exactly the *opposite*. They generate feelings of security, comfort and peace. They also instill a greater sense of self-respect in us and in those we love.

So, while I know you'd sometimes like to, don't give up! The methods and tips outlined in this book will help you set clear boundaries. They'll also serve as points of discussion which get each of your stepfamily members thinking and talking about ways you can improve your lives. Pretty soon, you'll all enjoy healthier, happier and more peaceful relationships with yourselves and one another. The key is taking it one "step" at a time!

Warmly,
Claudette

Claudette Chenevert
The Stepmom Coach
Claudette@StepmomCoach.com

INTRODUCTION

> *"Good fences make good neighbors." – Robert Frost, from the poem "Mending Wall" (1914)*

Why a book on boundaries when, as stepmoms, we have little say in such matters? That's precisely why!

Even as a child I knew that, if I didn't feel a sense of clear boundaries around me, I was likely to push my parents' buttons just to see how far I could get. I had an insatiable desire to find out what would happen if I tried *this* or *that*, meaning find some way to get into trouble. There were other times I knew right off the bat that, if I even dared to cross a line, I'd wind up in big trouble. In cases like those, I wouldn't even get close to approaching any lines my parents had drawn. Then there were the moments in which my parents wouldn't say a peep. Like the time I argued with my mother about some trivial thing, telling her she didn't know what she was talking about.

Neither of my parents said a word. For me, it signaled that I needed to continue with my argument to see how far I could take it. All of a sudden, my father got up and *whacked* me across the mouth. I guess I'd crossed a boundary I hadn't seen coming. I knew, both in my head and in my heart, that I might be pushing it. Yet, who was stopping me? For the most part, no one. I wanted someone to tell me, "Enough! If you go on with this kind of behavior, here's what's going to happen to you." What I wanted (most of all) was for someone to parent me: to stop me when I misbehaved and to show me where, in fact, my willfulness should end and the line around decorum began.

When I became a parent and then a stepparent, teaching boundaries to our kids held new importance. Still, it was difficult and challenging. It's one thing to set boundaries and another to enforce them, especially when it's essential that we do so. Not only that, but there's that little matter of delivering consequences at just the right time. When I began coaching other stepmoms, one of the most common issues they raised was setting boundaries: How do you go about it and how do you then enforce them? I'd sometimes recommend additional reading, though I found that any books available to moms and stepmoms didn't directly answer those questions—either for them or for me.

Some of those titles were heavily based on biblical teachings. This made them difficult to read among clients who didn't have strong religious beliefs or underpinnings. Others made only passing references to boundaries in their discussions of other topics or concepts. In truth, boundaries truly are part of a greater whole. As with anything, building and creating a family (or, in this case, a stepfamily) requires many different skill sets. Mastering boundaries is just one part of the larger equation.

This book is the result of years spent reading, researching, interacting with clients, asking questions, journeying through self-discovery myself and gaining experience through good old trial and error. While I don't claim to believe that it will teach you every single thing you need to know about boundaries over the course of a lifetime, I am confident in the fact that it's a strong starting point which *will* point you and your family in the right direction. As you begin to work through the material, know that the boundaries you create for your stepfamily will be informed by your own unique values and situation. No two homes are alike and so it goes for boundaries. You're the one who gets to decide what will work best for you—and what won't, given your stepfamily dynamic. Simply reading about boundaries will *not* be enough. You'll have to practice what you learn, in order to be effective.

To provide some help with that, I'm in the process of creating a companion program which I hope will deepen your understanding of boundaries and give you the extra boost of confidence needed to make related decisions. In the end, your boundaries will be your own. What one person takes issue with may not mean all that much to you. We see this play out in our stepfamilies, which are filled with various perspectives on what's acceptable and what's not. We all have different parenting styles, too. As a stepmom, you might take issue with your stepkids leaving their dirty dishes in the sink or on the counter. Maybe you feel as if they could have just as easily put them in the dishwasher. Your spouse, however, doesn't see it as a big deal. He may even tell you to put the dishes in the dishwasher yourself, if it bothers you so much.

What we're really talking about here are feelings. You want to be valued and respected. Dirty dishes left out in plain sight are a visual reminder, for you, that you're neither valued nor respected. Because this issue is important to you but not your spouse, you feel as if he fails to validate your feelings. This, by the way, illustrates the contribution biological parents make to setting boundaries. When those parents defend their children's actions rather than address them, we feel even more powerless. Whether they do it out of guilt or shame, their desire to avoid disciplining their children and to avoid confrontation with those children (or their exes) can make us feel woefully alone in our fight to draw clear and immovable lines.

Kids are known to test parental will, pushing our buttons and seeing how far they can get. Every time a boundary gets moved, they feel encouraged to move it even farther. That is, until their parents stand up and say, "Enough!" The longer you wait to deal with problems and issues like these, the more difficult they become to correct. Children soon believe this is how it's supposed to be, since they suffer no consequences. As you can see, boundary issues involving children don't always indicate that you have a problem child on your hands. Parents must learn to put boundaries in place and then be willing to enforce them. Guilt isn't reason enough to give them free rein.

As someone standing on the outside looking in—with the perspective *only* a stepmom is privy to—you can see how a lack of boundaries is causing your family a lot of grief; some, if not all of it, unnecessary. You yearn for the day when mutual respect and validation are enjoyed by everyone in your stepfamily. You also have a right to expect that the members of your household adhere to basic rules and conduct themselves in ways which will make you all healthier and happier. Will they resist? Maybe. Boundaries aren't easily put in place.

Yet, this I know: *The rewards are worth it!*

PART ONE

What are ... boundaries?
Why are they needed? And how can you
get your stepfamily to embrace change, as you
and your partner strive to make everyone's lives
easier? This section answers those questions
and others. You can *both* set boundaries
effectively and confidently. Find
out how, by turning
a new page
now

CHAPTER 1

What Are Boundaries?

> "A boundary is saying, explicitly: 'Here's what is okay and here's what is not okay.'" – Brené Brown, PhD, in "Boundary Setting Deep Dive" (2015)

Research professor, author and public speaker Brené Brown, PhD, LMSW, is known for work which focuses largely on the study of traits and emotions the stepmom population can readily relate to: courage, vulnerability, shame and empathy. Her book titles include *The Gifts of Imperfection, Daring Greatly* and *Dare to Lead: Brave Work. Tough Conversations. Whole Hearts.*

Brown views vulnerability as the ultimate brave act. In her words, it's "the willingness to be 'all in' even when you know it" may lead to failure or hurt feelings. In her "Boundary Setting Deep Dive" e-course, Brown also shares what she believes boundaries truly are. Rather than serve as a series of lines drawn in the sand which tell others what they're *not* allowed to do, she suggests, they should serve as responsible behavioral guidelines between individuals. In that way, they represent limits around our personal space: physical, mental and emotional. These limits then communicate to others what we find acceptable and unacceptable.

Personally, I like to think of my own boundaries—and often ask my stepfamily coaching clients to imagine theirs—as being similar to a fence with a gate in it. Using your imagination, take a moment to envision a fence constructed around you. Its purpose is to keep unacceptable behaviors out while, at the same time, allowing you to let acceptable behaviors in. You're the one in charge of opening and closing that gate. You decide what or who gets through and what or who does not. You alone have the key to that gate, so it's up to you to be selective about if and when access will be granted. And to what or whom.

Further imagine that within the perimeter of your fence there's a yard with children playing in it. When they're fenced in, children use as much of the yard as possible. It's also common for them to test the fence's boundaries, seeing what happens when they either push or lean on it. Does it bend, break or hold up under the pressure? Within that fenced-in area, the children are free to explore. Knowing there are boundaries in place, they feel safe from and protected against what lies on the other side: insecurity and unpredictability. This reassurance allows them to thrive. The same holds true for you.

How do boundaries benefit us?

Within and outside of the stepfamily structure, boundaries help us determine who we are and help us differentiate our thoughts and feelings from those of other people (i.e., family, friends, strangers). They also help us establish a sense of closeness or distance in relation to our physical space and emotional capacity. This, in part, is why it's important to thoroughly consider your boundaries and to clearly define them. By knowing what your boundaries are, you'll also have an easier time navigating challenging moments which might involve your spouse, your stepkids, the ex and other key figures in your life. To truly benefit from the power of knowing your own boundaries, whenever possible and as appropriate, they should be clearly communicated. At a minimum, express them to your spouse/partner.

Still, while others may question your boundaries, this is an *inside* job. It's not up to anyone else (no, not even your spouse) to determine whether your boundaries make sense. Only you need to believe in them, since they typically reflect deeply held values and beliefs. They serve to defend and protect what you hold closest to your heart. Since our values and beliefs do change with time, as we evolve and grow, it's a good idea to periodically revisit them. This will allow you to widen or narrow your fenced-in territory and establish newer or more suitable boundaries which accommodate for a shift in circumstances. As you mature and your lifestyle changes, let your boundaries mature and change alongside you rather than insist that they remain firm. Leave room for your thoughts around them to ebb and flow, as well.

Think back to your single life. It's likely you rarely, if ever, had to share your bathroom with anyone else. Yet, all of a sudden, you now have a need to share that bathroom with your spouse and maybe your stepkids. You may feel a sense of discomfort over having someone else enter and utilize this once personal space. This is understandable, especially in your early years together, as you don't yet have a template for dealing with such emotions. Similarly, if your stepkids' friends simply walk into your home without knocking or ringing the doorbell, this might truly irk you. It's at points like these that you realize you need to set some boundaries around who's granted entry and how.

Until you're confronted with specific issues like these, you may not realize that boundaries around them are even necessary. Another way to look at it is this: Say you now live in your husband's home. By that I mean the one he and his children have shared, quite possibly with his ex-wife. It's common for a stepmom to want to modify the décor so that it suits her personal style and taste. She may even want to change the locks on the doors. Yet, when picking up the kids, your spouse's ex may have grown accustomed to simply entering that home at will.

Is your fence in need of mending?

It's reasonable to implement boundaries around if and when the ex might be invited (or, perhaps, welcomed) into your home and whether or not it's okay for her to roam around while she's there. This is also your home now and you're entitled to say, "No way!" to her intrusions. That doesn't mean you have to be confrontational in how you deal with such individuals or issues. Simply tell your spouse that you're not okay with the status quo and work together to remedy the problem. This is the point at which you and your partner need to be prepared to defend your territory, in order to enforce boundaries you've chosen to put in place together.

Things may begin to get a little tricky here. That's because we often wait to have our boundaries crossed, though we may have anticipated such events. When they *are* crossed, we and/or our partners aren't always willing to defend them. However, boundaries which are inconsistent are rarely enforceable. If one of your core values is to be respected, you can't allow your stepchild, the ex or anyone else to disrespect you without consequence. Remember that fence we mentioned earlier? If you don't make time to go around and ensure that it's standing firm and free of gaps—so that others are clear about where you begin and where they end—there can only be confusion over what's acceptable and what's not.

When setting boundaries, especially as they relate to your stepfamily, it helps to put a vision in place. How do you want your family to function? What elements make your family unique? Which issues do you struggle with most and need help dealing with? Where would boundaries come in handy? This book will come in handy, as it facilitates those conversations. As you move through subsequent chapters, you'll learn how to sit down with your partner and brainstorm ways you can both use boundaries to create the ideal family picture.

I'm not talking about pipe dreams here. I'm talking about creating a shared image, in your minds and on paper, of the best case scenario based on your unique stepfamily situation. You'll learn to refer to your values and beliefs, building a strong foundation upon which you can both add structure that benefits everyone in your home. Doing so yearly, for example, allows you to apply routine maintenance that keeps your stepfamily functioning well.

I can't tell you how many times clients have told me that, once they got married and dealt with the initial task of merging their families, they expected to simply sit back and enjoy their relationships. That'll never happen. As human beings, the one thing we can rely on is the fact that the way we view our relationships to the world around us, one another and ourselves will constantly change. Accepting and embracing this truth is a sure way to live a healthier, happier, more peace-filled life. So is adjusting your boundaries as your vision, goals, values or beliefs shift and begin to settle right alongside any dust that was kicked up when you first came together.

Will boundaries truly make you happier?

When we define what falls within our boundaries as an area in which we're able to feel and move about comfortably and safely, it's easy to see how establishing boundaries can improve: your outlook, your family members' outlooks, your couple's relationship, your home life and other domains. By attending to the physical, mental and emotional simultaneously, you get even closer to achieving happy, long-term outcomes for your entire stepfamily. The end goal should be to enjoy yourselves and each other more freely and without fear of abuse, judgment, injustice, disrespect, etc. You can expand that safe haven even farther, by using this book to decide upfront:

- What are you willing to accept?
- What are you not willing to accept?
- What will you tolerate, bear or put up with?

That last point of self-reflection deserves some clarification. Let's say your stepkids leave their backpacks laying in the foyer of your home without fail. Even though you don't like it, are you willing to tolerate, bear or put up with it? This is different from accepting it altogether or changing your opinion on the matter simply because it's a common occurrence. Whether they've been doing it for years, since well before you came onto the scene, is irrelevant.

If your entryway is wide and their backpacks are at least lined up against a wall, you may be able to tolerate this habit. If the backpacks are a trip hazard, mounting a coat rack your stepkids are expected to hang them on is a better solution. Why? That policy ensures everyone's safety and that's what healthy boundaries do: They encourage behaviors and thought processes which keep us and those around us safe from physical harm and undue emotional stress or strain.

One way this plays out in our daily lives is in the responsible use of our vehicles. When you put the key in the ignition and then drive down the street, you stay in your lane. Implicit is the statement, "I will not hit you." While setting boundaries for yourself and your own behavior, you're also protecting others.

Are everyone's boundaries the same?

Boundaries are expressions of who we are, what we appreciate and what we value. Similarly, they serve as expressions of who we aren't, what we don't appreciate and what we fail to see value in. When you have clear boundaries in place, they serve as outward extensions of your identity which teach people something about you. They do, in essence, some of the talking for you. It's likely you already have boundaries around things you find offensive: bodily noises at the dinner table, talking loudly, leaving wet towels on the bathroom floor and more.

Are everyone's boundaries—within or outside your stepfamily—the same? Certainly not. Often, though, our boundaries are tied to things we find it difficult to tolerate without taking action. When your teen stepdaughter yells at a younger brother for reading her diary, the offending child has crossed a very real boundary. One way to get kids to understand boundaries is to describe them as moats around medieval castles. These ditches are dug deep to keep others from infiltrating the kingdom. The only way to cross one is via a drawbridge controlled by the property owner. Its job is to make those on the inside feel as if they and their property are safe behind it.

When enlisting your partner's help with boundary setting, the analogy of a fence surrounding your home should work well. Remember, we're not talking about a wall here. With a fence, you can still see what's going on outside of it and other people can see in. You're not at all disconnected; you're simply separated by a barrier. As joint gatekeepers, you and your spouse share responsibility for keeping certain people and behaviors outside of your reach. You also control who gets close and what goes on within your home.

When either of you opens that gate, you must first ask yourselves: Why am I letting this person or behavior into our home/life and what will we gain or experience through this encounter? As primary gatekeepers, you're also tasked with letting other people know what you expect from them when they come to visit. When we neglect to set, communicate and enforce boundaries, we compromise the harmony and safety of everyone with our stepfamily systems. We invite in those who may be intent on stepping all over us, causing us pain and/or abusing our kindness. By being good stewards of your home, you teach people—from exes to stepkids—to show greater care and respect.

Get ready to set healthy boundaries!

As I stated earlier, boundaries play out differently for each of us. That's why, when you're dealing with a variety of personalities (such as when you're managing life within a stepfamily), it's critical to define what healthy boundaries look like. In the end, my goals are to help you and your stepfamily set boundaries which:

- Honor and respect your individuality.
- Clearly define what's acceptable—and not.
- Establish realistic guidelines and consequences.
- Breathe life into your stepfamily's values and beliefs.
- Increase your levels of trust, self-confidence and stability.

To give you something to work toward going forward, let's define healthy boundaries as invisible but well-defined dividing lines between what your stepfamily will accept, tolerate, believe and do—and not—which clarify what is and is not acceptable on three distinct levels: physical, mental (or psychological) and emotional.

Are you ready to get started? Me, too! Let's do this.

CHAPTER 2

What Boundaries Are Not

> "[A] boundary [is] the means by which a person seeks to organize and regulate their relationship with the world." – John Olesnavage, PhD, from Our Boundary (2009)

Boundaries are *not* the same as expectations.

Expectations are aspirational, according to Brené Brown. In fact, the word *expectation* derives from the Latin for "an awaiting." In this way, expectations are what we hope will happen at some point in the future. An expectation might include a strong belief you hold that your stepchild's or your partner's words and actions might one day sync up with your desires. Many stepmothers also expect, or hope, that one day their stepfamilies will come together with a minimum of conflict. After all, you and your partner love each other very much. This should be easy, right?

Well, that's not how it works. In the summer of 2018, my husband and I participated in "The Art and Science of Love" workshop at The Gottman Institute in Seattle. The program was created by the institute's founders, John M. Gottman, PhD, and Julie Schwartz Gottman, PhD, and was facilitated by Angela Voegele, LCSW. Part of what we learned, from the Gottmans' research, was that *all* couples experience conflict. Yep, every single one! The Gottmans believe that how you repair the conflict (which arises, say, from unmet expectations or unintended missteps) is what ultimately differentiates your relationship as one that's successful—and destined to last—from one that falls apart.

Because expectations are tied to hopes and beliefs, they're rife with assumptions and predictions which leave us feeling more like victims of circumstance than empowered and confident individuals. There's reason for that. Family, child and adult psychologist John Olesnavage, PhD, says people with rigid or incomplete boundaries "are unable to form healthy or lasting connections." (We'll discuss this in a later chapter.) As a result, he adds, their relationships are marked by incidents and issues involving control and dependency: "Over time, these relationships cause increased damage, as the person is forced to squash [his or her] true nature and compartmentalize happiness."

Sound familiar, stepmom? I bet it does. Stepmoms and the biological parents they're married to often opt to sacrifice their own identities and happiness for the sake of keeping the peace. In my work with stepfamilies, I've found this to be a way of life for stepmoms. They bite their tongues for fear they might offend their husbands. They live in homes which are shrouded in Daddy Guilt, where boundaries are either absent or difficult to enforce. They find themselves increasingly powerless to affect change and, at times, become highly depressed over the states of their households.

I want more for you. I'm sure you want more for yourself—and your stepfamily. When boundaries are properly created, they're clearly-defined. Appropriate consequences are attached to unwanted behaviors which then help each relationship within our family structures function well. Those boundaries are based on core values or beliefs we share with our spouses and family members. They make everyone within our homes feel safer and more secure. Related consequences fit the circumstances and aren't ever used to wield power or control over anyone else.

Expectations keep us mired in what might have been, whereas boundaries lead us to our best selves.

CHAPTER 3

Why We Need Boundaries

> *"[The] world can be an enormously confusing place for a child. So anything a parent can do to make it more manageable [or] 'decipherable' can be invaluable to a child's healthy development." –* Leon F. Seltzer, PhD, at Psychology Today online (2017)

A s I admitted earlier, when I was a child I used to push the boundaries of what was okay and what was *not* okay. However, as the eldest of four girls, I was often told that I was to set the example for my younger sisters. What I found most challenging, under those circumstances, was *not* knowing what my own boundaries were. I'd usually find out only after I had gone too far, which meant I might get a spanking, be sent to my room or worse. Still, I rarely got much of an explanation about what I had done that was wrong. Another problem with this was that my parents' boundaries were inconsistent.

There were days when I or all of us could get away with some of the worst behavior kids can carry out. For me, that included stuffing my youngest sister into a cupboard, locking it up and leaving her to figure out how she might get out of there. (She always did.) Other days, simply being too loud landed us in hot water and the consequences for that ranged from mild to severe. As a mother, a stepmother and a boundary-tester myself, I recognize and accept that it's normal for kids and stepkids to push our boundaries. As part of their developmental process, it's essentially their jobs. Yet, as adults, our jobs are to define and enforce boundaries in ways which keep our (step-)children from having to guess what acceptable behavior *is* and what it *isn't*.

It's up to us to let them know what our boundaries are and why we have them in place. It's not enough to say, "Because I said so!" Sure, there was a time when parents could get away with that. Our parents surely did! But it just doesn't hold true anymore. Kids are savvy nowadays. They've likely always been, though today they can scour the internet and compare notes with friends both near and far to see if what we're saying makes sense. Who can blame them? If I'd had access to a computer, when I was a child or a teen, I sure would have liked to have been able to do some research of my own.

Yet, why do we need boundaries? In a nutshell, boundaries help keep us safe. They keep us from being stepped on, manipulated and used. They let others know what's acceptable to us and what's not. They allow us to be ourselves, freely living our lives as we see fit. Additionally, they give definition and expression to: our own space, our own ideas, our own values and our own beliefs. When boundaries are clear, they provide others with a road map, or a set of directions, for how they are to behave around us. They're a line of demarcation between what we will and will not tolerate, but they're not always self-evident. In fact, they rarely are.

Let's say you have boundaries around respect:

- Does that mean we can't touch you?
- Does that mean we must call you Ma'am?
- Does it require direct eye contact when speaking to you?

As you can see from these examples, without a clear idea of what *respectful* behavior means to you, others will be unable to properly respect your boundaries around it. What's more, rather than in advance of it, it's in the midst of our discomfort that we often become aware that our boundaries have been crossed. Finally, though some boundaries appear to be universal ("You may not verbally, mentally or physically abuse me in any way."), some people ignore those basic and fundamental social boundaries either due to lack of experience or out of defiance.

As you begin setting boundaries which matter to you, guided by the help I'm offering here, focus on how you want others to treat you and to interact with you. For each topic, such as respectful behavior, dig deep and clearly outline what you consider to be acceptable and unacceptable. Your own level of acceptance will surely differ from your spouse's and your stepkids', so don't leave any detail open to interpretation. If you aren't clear in your communication about what it is you need, you can't expect anyone else to clearly understand it, either.

Let's talk a bit about tolerance.

I'd like to share a quick word about tolerance with you. Tolerance is the ability or willingness to allow an issue, problem or situation to be exactly what it is without any request or demand for change. This is especially true in situations where a given opinion or behavior fails to strike a chord with you based on your own values and beliefs. For example, your spouse may never put dirty dishes in the dishwasher and your stepkids may never clean their rooms. If you're willing to tolerate this behavior, you simply accept that it's their way of being in the world and adjust your own thinking and behavior to allow for this. Yet, no relationship ever stays the same.

All relationships experience ebb and flow. Some days may seem great! Other days the challenges we face can make us question those relationships' importance or relevance to us. If your home is cluttered with dirty dishes and you seem to be the only one who cares, your tolerance level will fluctuate. Suddenly, what once didn't seem quite so important is now an issue that's driving you mad. Why can't they rinse their dirty dishes and put them in the dishwasher—like you do?! By failing to set a boundary in the first place, you've set a precedent.

This doesn't mean you can't ever change your mind or put that boundary in place. What it's proof of is that, when things are going well in our relationships, we're usually reluctant to "dredge up" what's bothering us or to talk about changes we'd like to see happen. When our relationships are *not* going well, however, we begin to view change as inevitable. If we feel discontent, we view it as a sign that we need to have a little talk. Hey, it's also possible you've avoided the topic of boundaries because you believe they should be clear to others. It could even be that you think you know what your partner's boundaries are or what your (step-)children's boundaries are. But, do you? Really?

Truth is, unless you've had a conversation around expectations and boundaries, you can't be sure. You're assuming you know, which leaves ample room for misinterpretation or false understanding. Having a conversation around boundaries doesn't mean that every conversation you have should revolve around this. Still, if you never talk about what's important or acceptable to you, you run the risk of reaching maximum tolerance and contributing to a blowup that won't make you or those around you feel cared for or understood.

Putting boundaries in place, in advance, ensures that your needs will and can be met in a timely way.

CHAPTER 4

What Experts Say About Boundaries

> "[Stepfamilies which were] open with their feelings, directly addressed conflict and reframed their conflict in a positive way were able to manage the conflict and power imbalances in their [families]." – Tamara D. Afifi, from the Journal of Social and Personal Relationships (2003)

Rules. Boundaries. We all live by them! They're built into the frameworks of our societies and our communities. School is a great example, especially for kids. Without boundaries in our school systems our children's experiences of them would be chaotic. Imagine, for a minute, a world in which there are no rules or boundaries. What does that look like? No one would be at work on time, if people actually worked. Kids wouldn't learn anything at school, too busy goofing off to read or write. People would feel free to come in and out of our homes, whenever they pleased.

Essentially, our lives would be a jumbled mess. Boundaries establish order in society, as a whole, and in the home. They create structure. They contribute to our sense of security and belonging, since we know what to expect of others. Boundaries help us live and function within our families and our communities. Consequences are an important aspect of boundary setting which, once established, provide adults and children with cues for addressing issues and problems as they arise. At the very least, they serve as guidelines for dealing with those things.

Similarly, House Rules provide guidelines for our stepfamilies. The *best* House Rules instill a sense of fairness and encourage teamwork. The *worst* instill fear or apprehension over the power and influence held by parents and stepparents. Your ability to create clear, relevant, fair and consistent family rules which are enforceable and are then enforced helps determine the quality and strength of your marriage and your other stepfamily relationships. (Now, isn't that worth looking into?) That's why, as your stepfamily merges, it's important to set boundaries early on.

While thoughtfully establishing new roles for yourselves and new norms may help you forge a new family identity, proceed with caution here. Due to loyalty binds, you must have your spouse's support—or your stepkids may rally against you to preserve their notions of family identity, which to some degree still involve their mother—and you should resist turning everyone's world upside down simply because you've now joined forces. On a related note, it's also important to have a family discussion about what it's *okay* to discuss with others (i.e., Mom) and what should remain private. Without clear communication, you can't be assured of confidentiality within your stepfamily home.

Every member of your stepfamily plays a role in fostering a sense of trust and intimacy, finds Tamara D. Afifi, PhD, who's a professor of communication at the University of California in Santa Barbara. In "'Feeling Caught' in Stepfamilies: Managing Boundary Turbulence through Appropriate Communication Privacy Rules," she notes that after relationships end (via divorce or separation) each member of the former couple's individual boundaries need to be redefined, especially as they pertain to what sorts of information will be shared between them and their children.

What does research reveal about boundaries?

Healthy boundaries contribute to a sense of security, comfort, serenity and self-respect in the relationships we have with ourselves and with others. They attract to us the types of experiences we can live with and keep those we want to avoid at bay. They give expression to our unique, individual personalities. Reflect, for a minute, on your own family of origin. At one point or another, most of its members—including you—learned to set and hold firm to certain boundaries. Those sorts of boundaries give definition to what's collectively considered acceptable or unacceptable within that family system. It's no different for your stepfamily.

Boundaries also play a role in regulating our emotional and physical well-being. For example: "I don't want to walk down that alleyway. It's much too dark." They regulate our health, too, such as when we decide, "I can't possibly eat chips and drink cola for breakfast. It's not good for my body." In addition, they contribute to any emotional distance or intimacy which exists between us and others: "I can't visit you; it's very uncomfortable when you let your dogs jump all over me," or, "Jim, I need time to think about this. Do you mind leaving me alone for a bit?"

Afifi's work on the communication styles of successful stepfamilies has a lot to teach us. Drawing on the prior research of a variety of experts from multiple disciplines, she gleaned numerous insights into best practices which you and your partner would be wise to adopt, as you go about setting and then enforcing boundaries on behalf of your entire stepfamily. My hope is that, by arming yourselves with expert opinions on the matter, you'll be better equipped to understand the critical role boundaries play in your stepfamily and to set rules around communication.

(10) *of her most important findings, in my view, are summarized here:*

- Unified fronts deter loyalty conflicts.
- Openness fosters stepfamily solidarity.
- It's healthier to share facts than keep secrets.
- Respect for information privacy is paramount.
- Rules and boundaries over info sharing must exist.
- Communicating openly prevents power imbalances.
- Dad should underscore stepmom's role and authority.
- Dad should stand behind the couple's relationship, too.
- It is better to acknowledge problems than deny they exist.
- Positively addressing conflict/feelings directly solves issues.

Keeping stepfamily communication boundaries in place does require a coordinated effort on everyone's part. This is particularly important given that one person's missteps can invariably impact your entire family. Afifi found, for one, that "former spouses who relay too much personal information to one another may create confusion" for and incite jealousy in stepparents, who often struggle to define and understand biological parents' ongoing relationships.

In sum total, her research showed that stepfamily members can enjoy cohesive, cooperative relationships with one another. Holding onto realistic expectations and allowing your interpersonal bonds to develop naturally are two ways you can achieve that. Others include allowing individuals to share information with one another at a pace they find comfortable (as in, one which doesn't infringe on their own boundaries around privacy) and striking a balance between what's considered public information versus what you, your partner and your stepkids might keep private.

It's time you and your stepfamily benefited from that and related wisdom.

CHAPTER 5

What Purpose Do Boundaries Serve?

> *"I was slowly letting go of personal boundaries in favor of keeping the peace, whatever that meant. I wasn't so sure anymore, since I felt anything but peaceful." – Kelly Seal, from "A Lesson in Creating Boundaries" at Huff Post (2011)*

Boundaries serve a number of different purposes. For one thing, they actually build trust between you and the people you interact with most: your partner, your stepkids, your own immediate family, extended family members who play significant roles in your lives and, ideally, any exes you and/or your spouse have a need to deal with on a regular basis. They do that by establishing a baseline for consistent behavior. In other words, when people know they can rely on you to stay true to your word and vice versa, it becomes easier to trust one another. What a relief that is!

For another, boundaries help us build up our self-confidence. Being able to get your wants and needs met—by simply standing up for yourself and firmly saying, "No," when someone tries to cross a boundary with you or when you just plain old mean it—is empowering. Furthermore, having clearly defined boundaries in place helps us relax more and hold those who show support for the limits we've set in a more favorable light. This is a much healthier way to approach the day, knowing you needn't be on high alert at every turn.

My grandkids are a great example of firm but loving boundaries in action. When they come to our home for a sleepover, they know exactly what to expect from us and exactly what our rules are. As a result, we never have any issues with them or their behaviors. They know that: What we say, we mean. They are unable to push our buttons, because there are *no* buttons to push! Our grandkids clearly know what they can and cannot do. Their parents are often surprised at how well-behaved they are in our home, especially when it comes time for them to eat, play or sleep.

As a happy side effect of standing firm, as stepmoms, all of a sudden exes learn to resist that urge to berate us. Our stepkids stop being quite so disrespectful, as well. That's because they know and understand what it is we value and believe. By now, they've gotten a taste of the consequences they'll face if they choose to continually ignore or trample on our values and beliefs. It's important to note here that, in order for a boundary to be truly respected, it helps if the other person (your stepson or stepdaughter, say) finds merit in it or has a stake in it somehow.

So, if you learn only one thing in this chapter, make it this: When people are free to disagree, they are free to love. When they are instead forced into agreement or shamed for their own values and beliefs, they live in fear and their concept of love becomes damaged or distorted. When it comes to your stepfamily, setting boundaries with love in your heart is extremely important. This isn't a dictatorship. Boundaries aren't intended to fix, change or punish anyone. They're intended to teach us all a little something about self-care, nurturing behavior and mutual respect.

Let's say your stepson has made a habit of leaving his clean and dirty clothes strewn around his room. Over and over again, you and your husband have asked him to put his clean clothes in his drawers or closet. By letting him know that he'll now be responsible for his own laundry, until he chooses to pick up his room, you put the onus back on him. You also give him the freedom to live in a messy room, as long as he keeps the door shut. You're being considerate of his choice to live in a messy room and you're also being fair to yourself. Regarding this, I tell clients, "The ball is now in your stepchild's court. He can either serve it or let it fall flat at his feet."

The likelihood that he'll now more readily follow through on your wishes just increased along with his respect for you—which will be even more evident once he realizes that his soccer shorts or favorite pair of jeans have gone "missing." More importantly, you'll now have less to stress over and less to argue about with your husband. Any younger siblings who are living or staying in your home are also likely to take note. Heck, everyone's stress levels decrease when they understand where the line is drawn and know what's likely to happen when it's crossed.

That is, as long as you don't give in. Don't try to "save" him from wearing dirty, smelly, rumpled clothes. Remember: If your stepchild decides *not* to put away his or her clean laundry, your stepchild is also making the decision to live with the consequences. Don't take that decision personally. You're not a bad stepparent. It's also okay to feel uncomfortable about the situation. Be uncomfortable! Hopefully, so will your stepchild. This may be just what's needed to motivate them to make better decisions and to respect the rules of your home going forward.

As we talked about in earlier chapters, boundaries help you:

- Regain control over your life.
- Create a more stable home life.
- Stay true to your own values/beliefs.
- Take ownership of your personal space.
- Set limits on people's behavior toward you.

Boundaries play a large role in helping us distinguish between codependency and interdependency, too. Codependency can be debilitating, as it causes us to look outside of ourselves for reassurance, instruction and/or validation. It's what leads one parent to rely on a child to serve as a messenger between homes or to take on adult responsibilities at a young age. By contrast, interdependency is a healthy sharing of ideas and burdens between spouses, family members and others who comprise our stepfamily support systems.

What about boundaries for stepkids?

When you and/or your partner set boundaries with the intention of empowering your (step-)kids, you help them gain a much needed sense of autonomy. This helps them individuate and distinguish themselves as someone other than your stepson, their father's offspring or their mother's baby boy. A healthy sense of self is critical to successful child development and to teens' transition into adulthood. Without it, making decisions and making it on their own will be tasks they'll find difficult to master. Knowing what is and is not acceptable will benefit them in the real world; the one which awaits them outside your door.

Now, there are parents who would rather not have their children individuate. Those parents typically feel as if they are "losing" their children who, for quite a while, have given them a sense of identity. Moms, maybe due to social pressure, tend to create a world around themselves that's based on being The Mom/The One who

26

takes care of her children. They view their children as part of themselves rather than as individuals who'll one day leave home to start families of their own. That level of emotional attachment can leave children feeling responsible for their parents' well-being or emotional security rather than vice versa.

Back to you now. Perhaps you won't allow your stepkids to cuss in your home. Or, maybe, their other parent allows them to drink alcohol on special occasions—at a family member's wedding reception, for example. That first one may not result in your stepchildren breaking any laws, though they may serve time in detention for cussing at school. The second scenario is more likely to land them in trouble, if they're young teens who wind up driving home drunk after the festivities. In either case, as a stepparent, model the behaviors you expect from your stepkids.

You have absolutely no control over what happens at their other parent's house. Nor should you try to, as it would be hypocritical to overstep a very real boundary into the other home's territory. What is important, however, is to set rules and boundaries in your home which are consistent with your values or beliefs and are then enforced. After all, there's no point in creating boundaries if you aren't going to enforce them or attach consequences to them. The more clear their choices are ("If you choose to ____, ____ will happen."), the more responsible you force them to become.

In the introduction to this book and in other chapters, I shared with you my own personal history with boundaries. The rules, limits and boundaries in the family home I grew up in were unclear. I pushed, prodded and tested them at every turn. I did this hoping to find out what my limits actually were. I'm not alone in that. Across the board, children crave rules, limits and boundaries. They want to know what your family's boundaries are, so they can feel a sense of security and protection.

They also benefit from learning to recognize the correlation between actions and outcomes. Whether they view the resulting consequence as good or bad, the guidance you provide by setting firm boundaries for your own kids or for your stepkids will help them function more healthfully within your family and within society. The structure you provide them with now will also serve to minimize any unnecessary stress and chaos your family experiences in the home, by giving each of you a clear understanding of what's expected ... and what to expect.

The way you engage with one another—as you begin to set boundaries which are unique to your own home—goes a long way toward showing them how it is you'd like to be treated, in return. So, do make a point of modeling the behaviors you hope to see expressed by the other members of your stepfamily.

You'll be glad you did!

CHAPTER 6

What Sorts of Boundaries Are There?

> *"Social skills coaching [for kids] is always best when you can do it in real time. They're more likely to remember what to do in that situation and be able to replicate the behavior next time it comes up." – Mandi Silverman, from "Teaching Kids about Boundaries" at Child Mind Institute*

Whenever we consider boundaries, it's important to note that respect for other people—regardless of who they are—should serve as our foundation for creating them. It's never okay to degrade, abase, humiliate or denigrate others; not even if that's what they're doing to you. If a person does treat you in this fashion, you have the option to tell them to stop and to let them know that their behavior is unacceptable and that, furthermore, you won't tolerate it.

Then, ask to be treated with dignity and respect. If the other person (i.e., a spouse who's angry, a stepkid who's being disrespectful, an ex who's spewing venom) refuses, let them know you're done with the conversation and will return to it at a more appropriate time. As in, when you're both able to have a civil conversation around the issue. Under no circumstances must you tolerate or endure inappropriate behavior which puts you in emotional, physical or psychological danger. This raises the topic of boundaries types.

There are (3) basic boundary types:

- Rigid
- Weak
- Healthy

Rigid boundaries can be identified pretty easily. In this situation, a person says, "No" to practically everything. They essentially cut themselves off from any kind of relationship, activity or experience—even if it might add fun or joy to their lives. They are basically saying, "No," to life itself. Their boundaries are so rigid that it seems as if they've secluded themselves behind a brick wall that not even a pickaxe could penetrate.

That's how I once behaved, when it came to my stepdaughters. I was so afraid of being hurt, of not measuring up to their expectations and of failing to be the stepmom they wanted (or, perhaps, needed) me to be that I shut myself out behind this façade and allowed only my son and my husband to access the real me. I was determined not to let anyone hurt me ever again. Yet, one day, my husband told me he was tired of trying to chip away at my wall.

If I didn't let the world in, he said, he wouldn't be able to stick around much longer. I was shocked! I hadn't realized just how much I had shut myself off from others; all in order to protect myself from being hurt. I had isolated myself to the point that I was pushing everyone away. I'd thought that being rigid would give me greater control over my life but realized that I wasn't truly living, either. I had to be willing to feel disappointment, sadness, fear, anger, etc.

Weak boundaries are less specific. Here, we're talking about the person who *can't* say, "No," to anyone or anything. They become the doormat of the family and other social spheres: The Pushover. This is essentially the other side of the rigid boundaries coin. Someone with weak boundaries may say, "Yes," to keep the peace. They may say, "Yes," because they're unsure of themselves. Dad may do this, feeling guilty for "breaking up the family" his kids once shared with him. As with rigid boundary types, these people feel alone and isolated.

They don't have relationships based on trust and intimacy, as they're often taken advantage of. Others think, "Hmmm, how much can I get out of them?" We often see weak boundaries in so-called Disney Moms and Dads who—whether their children are with them for the day, the weekend, winter break or an entire summer—agree to just about anything. They do this out of a fear of disappointing, being rejected by or being pushed away by their kids. Their self-esteem and self-worth are both tied up in what they're able to give to others. As a result, their sense of worth and well-being are askew.

People who set healthy boundaries often offer up a mix of yeses and nos. They clearly understand what motivates their responses, since their boundaries are deeply rooted in their values and beliefs. They know what it is they envision for themselves and for their families. They also accept that the kids will test, resist and try to break through family boundaries. Either as a parent or a stepparent, these people make no qualms about firmly and respectfully reminding the children what the household boundaries are and why they exist.

What else should you know about boundaries?

There are (3) main categories of boundaries, related to:

- *Personal Space* – "Please, no. I don't enjoy being touched."
- *Adult/Child Relations* – "Carrie, your dad and I need some privacy."
- *Household/Group Behavior* – "I won't tolerate your ex acting as if this is her home."

Bear those in mind, as you consider ways in which you can construct boundaries for acceptable behavior within your own stepfamily home. A few domains you might want to consider, as we move forward, include:

- Your bedroom
- Sibling bedrooms
- Other private spaces
- Interpersonal interaction
- Interpersonal communication

When children and stepchildren are of the opposite sex or new to the family, putting boundaries in place around access to other sibling bedrooms is key. This is especially true when they're different ages (i.e., toddler, adolescent, teen), since the amount of privacy they want, need and are entitled to differ. When it comes to other areas of the home—such as the couple's bathroom or anything other than the family living room—do you want the ex to be able to access them? Probably not. What about the kids' bedrooms? If she can then access other private spaces, uh, "No."

Privacy is just one area of conflict that's common among stepfamilies. Yet, you also need to ask yourself how you'd like to be treated and spoken to. What's acceptable with regard to interpersonal behavior or conversation? What's not? Is a playful nudge okay? Should some topics be taboo at the dinner table? As you consider these things, notice how you feel about them and acknowledge that. This will empower you to do what's right for you. We teach people how to treat and interact with us. Giving expression to your limits is part of the boundary-setting process, whereas not saying anything at all is the same as giving away your personal power. You have a voice. Use it!

We'll delve into this next topic in greater detail as the second section of this book unfolds. Still, I'd like you to start thinking about how and where you draw the line when it comes to sharing information between your home and the other home your stepkids and/or own kids spend their time at. One way families sometimes connect is by keeping "family secrets." At times, this can be a good thing. (Hey, you may not want mom knowing that you dye your hair!)

At other times, it can have negative results. Let's say a parent or other relative is suffering from emotional or drug-related problems. The other members of their family will have a tendency to keep this secret tightly under wraps. The same can be said of sexual abuse. Often, what keeps people from sharing word of these experiences is the shame associated with the problem. A boundary then shoots up over who gets to know about the issue and who doesn't. We can probably agree that, in instances like these, we'd want to know what's going on.

What happens, in reality, is that any preexisting wedge between biological parents and stepparents grows larger and now keeps us from being privy to important information of this sort. In addition, it's common for stepparents to already be excluded from difficult "family" conversations based on the outdated premise that they aren't "part of the (original) family." Given all of that, these sorts of issues can be difficult to recognize, assess and address.

Yet, whenever a person's life or welfare is in danger, it should always be brought to the attention of someone who's in a position of authority and can be trusted to do the right thing: you, your partner, an outside agency, etc. Communicate this to the children, so that they know they can rely on you to help them navigate tough challenges and are not alone. Let them know that sexual and emotional abuse are *not* to be tolerated. While they may have learned that saying, "No," to their elders is a bad thing which can get them into trouble, this is an exception.

Finally, help them understand that any information they share with you will be held in strict confidence whenever possible. Lead by example. One way to do that is to avoid oversharing intimate details of your own life (such as past regrets or recurring arguments you and your spouse have) with others. That includes your own kids, your stepkids, the ex, acquaintances and other stepmoms or moms you've met on the soccer field.

Oversharing is a sign of inadequate boundaries—plain and simple.

PART TWO

Are you ... ready to go?
Let's dig in—helping you, you partner
and your (step-)children set boundaries you
can truly live with. A healthier, happier, more
peaceful home life awaits! Use these time-
tested tips and targeted exercises to
address common problem
areas. Grow closer,
as you do it,
too!

CHAPTER 7

Setting Personal & Physical Boundaries

Why all the conflict? Turns out, there is a reason for it. If your boundaries, those of your partner and/or those of any children involved seem to be out of sync, take heart. Whether we're aware of it or not, each of us already has a set of boundaries in place which are based largely on our values. Those values reflect our upbringings, as well as what we learned as young adults when we began navigating the world outside our homes of origin and before settling into routines or environments of our own choosing.

When we then form first families or stepfamilies of our own, those values come with us—neatly or hastily boxed up with our personal belongings. It's those preexisting values which nudge us to put related guidelines in place; ones we hope will help us establish and manage the cultures we seek to create within our own homes. The problem occurs when people disagree over what is right and what is wrong. We begin to judge our interactions as being good vs. bad, safe vs. dangerous and better vs. worse. The urge to compare our value systems to others' is innate, yet we each possess a different and distinct set of values.

Given that, is it even possible to reach a compromise that works for everyone? Whether you and your spouse are just merging your two families or have been at it for years, there's a good chance your values and boundaries continue to collide. After all, you entered into this union with different backgrounds, different upbringings and different cultural views. Simply acknowledging this is a great first step toward reaching a level of compromise you can all live with. I'm living proof. (I may be a stepfamily professional but I'm human, too.) My husband, Bernard, and I struggled to find middle ground. So did our kids. Eventually? We did. You can, too.

The remainder of this book offers information and exercises which will help you do just that!

What boundaries do you find acceptable?

The two areas I recommend tackling first are *Personal Boundaries* and *Physical Boundaries*. That's because they work hand-in-hand to establish a framework for setting and holding fast to boundaries which affect every other aspect of your life: home, work, community, etc. Each one is covered in detail below but, in order to get you thinking about how they might impact you and your stepfamily on a regular basis, I've offered up a quick list of personal and physical domains it's worth mulling over upfront.

Consider how boundaries currently affect:

- Your couple's relationship (incl. private time)
- Your bedroom & your kids' bedrooms
- Your stuff: car, jewelry, clothing, etc.
- Your shared stepfamily home
- Your physical body

What are your boundaries around these things today? Make a paper or electronic list and jot down at least one boundary you currently have in place for each of these areas. When it comes to your couple's relationship, is it important that his cell phone is turned off during sex—so you won't be interrupted by texts from his kids or his ex? When it comes to your bedroom and those of the kids, is it a free-for-all or are they off limits to everyone else? When it comes to your stuff, are your stepkids allowed to root around at will? When it comes to your home, is the ex required to wait for her kids in the doorway or foyer? You get the idea.

What this list will help you do is assess where you're at and, eventually, where you want to end up. It's always a good idea to revisit your list of boundaries from time to time. That's because what you find non-negotiable today may change with time. As your stepdaughters become teens, you may be thrilled at the idea of them wanting to wear your clothing—or not—like those jeans you keep saving, in the hopes that you'll one day fit back into them. None of these should be set in stone, as the nature and quality of your relationships with one another will fluctuate.

While you're at it, ask your partner and maybe even the kids to draft initial lists of their own. Knowing where each of you draws the line on these issues will give you a better understanding of where some of that conflict I mentioned earlier stems from. Do this at a time when your relationships are experiencing a sense of calm and things are going well. The same rule applies to setting newer and (here's hoping) healthier boundaries. That way, when difficult times or moments set in, you'll already have guidelines in place for interacting over and solving them.

Let's get back to your own list. After drafting it, review it again. For each item, think of an example when your boundary around it was *respected*. Then, think of a time when it wasn't. As you reflect back, notice how you feel now. Write down your feelings, if you like. This process will empower you to: Recognize the event as having passed, accept either outcome and make deliberate decisions going forward. Remember, we teach people how to treat us. Expressing yourself is part of the boundary-setting process. Getting clear on what you can live with (and what you cannot) is central to that.

Setting boundaries at home will eventually help you set and enforce boundaries in every area of your life, rather than stew over transgressions you perceive to be injustices. Unless you communicate your wishes, no one else will be privy to them. Getting clear is also a way to shore up your personal power, especially if you compare it to flying by the seat of your pants. Doing the latter diminishes your personal power and is likely to make you angry at others or over circumstances you can't control but can certainly set clear, communicated limits around.

Imagine going to work and suddenly finding out that your job duties and responsibilities have changed drastically. Or that you were transferred (without first being consulted) to an office 60 miles farther from home. Would you be confused? Upset? Outraged? Your partner, children and stepchildren might react similarly if one day they came home and suddenly all of the rules had changed—yet you'd failed to, in advance, communicate that or provide them with a reason why. Any decisions about boundaries you make mentally need to be communicated verbally.

True story: While my mom was in intensive care after giving birth to a three-month-premature baby, my father decided to move our family from the city to an out-of-the-way place where only French was spoken. Though she was French Canadian, my mom spoke only English. When Mom left the hospital, only then did he tell her, "Oh, by the way, we moved. Welcome home!?"

It's not uncommon for stepchildren who divide their time between two homes (which can also mean two sets of friends, pets, belongings and more) to already feel confused, upset and outraged. Can you blame them? Everything they once knew, valued and relied on has been upended. I encourage you to develop empathy for the way everyone in your home is affected by stepfamily life. It's not just you who's been put upon on or been put in a situation that's unfamiliar. It's all of you. Moving forward, I ask that you remain open to the possibility that the information you glean and exercises you take part in have the distinct possibility of increasing your stepfamily's solidarity.

At this point you know, at least to some extent, what you're starting with. You know where it is you'd like to steer your stepfamily, since you're now aiming for greater cohesion. You know that your relationships will ebb and flow, requiring you to be flexible. You also know that a boundary which exists *only* in your mind isn't one you can expect others to adhere to. As you begin to guide your stepfamily on a path to infinitely better boundaries: Foster a sense of openness, encourage communication and adopt a teamwork mentality. Behave in ways which show a willingness to leave the conflict behind you, so you can all move forward together.

Personal Boundaries

Personal boundaries are the guidelines, rules and limits we've set for ourselves regarding our relationships with others. They typically stem from what it is we believe or have found to be: reasonable, safe and permissible ways for other people to behave around us. They also provide us with an internal blueprint for responding, either through our words or our actions, when someone steps outside of those limits and makes us feel unsafe or insecure.

Teens often set personal boundaries around their parents and siblings, as a way of establishing identities of their own. Children of divorce, in general, can be said to be highly protective of their personal boundaries. We see this when it comes to discussions involving their biological parents—a phenomenon that, in part, inflames or reinforces loyalty binds which can make it difficult for stepmoms to assimilate and establish a sense of belonging in their own homes. It can feel as if a circle is drawn around the original, nuclear family and you're left standing outside of it.

A strong couple's relationship and dad's willingness to acknowledge both you and the importance of your new relationship are two ways to combat this. Feeling caught in the middle (i.e., a child between his mom and dad, a husband between his wife and kids) may signal that someone's personal boundaries were violated or disrespected. We see this play out for dads who are trying to simultaneously support their new wives, please their kids and appease their ex-wives. There is a sense that, no matter what they do, their decisions will never be appropriate or measure up as "good enough" from at least one person's perspective: his wife's, his child's or his ex's.

The sensation of feeling fenced in by a variety of opinions leaves them feeling as if there's nowhere to go but down. The more those fences close in on us, the more frustrated we become. As a result, anger and fear begin to guide our decisions; often, in direct opposition to our personal values, beliefs, family visions and/or goals. The thought of enjoying strong and healthy relationships can seem like a fantasy. Yet, in particular, our visions and goals are what help us frame our lives and picture what it would be like to create circumstances of our own imagining. They also provide us with the motivation and direction necessary to attain them.

It's important to note, here, that our definition of *self* is often impacted by our relationships with others. We don't define who we are from within a vacuum; we do it in relationship to others. Take, for example, Alice. She's a stepmom coaching client of mine who was trying to build a relationship with her stepdaughter. All of her prior experiences with young girls were positive, including participation in a Big Sister program which Alice enjoyed immensely. Yet, those experiences weren't nearly as intimate as the ones she encountered with her husband's daughter. None of those other girls had lived with her or had a need to "share" their father with her. In defining her stepmom role, Alice needed to account for her stepdaughter's personal boundaries and previously established relationships with her biological father and mother. Alice's sense of self, in this context, was challenged.

The larger your stepfamily, the more challenging your own situation may be. One way to make it easier to define your role within your stepfamily is to recognize that it's up to you to set and maintain a view of yourself that reflects precisely who it is you *know* yourself to be. In other words, don't let who you are or how you view yourself be warped in response to how your spouse, stepkids or anyone else responds to you. Healthy personal boundaries result in a healthy sense of self; one that's distinct and, therefore, prevents you from becoming either enmeshed in or encumbered by others' wants, needs, desires or identities.

You will know you're enmeshed when your personal boundaries are so entwined with those of others that the line between who you are and who they are is blurred. In addition, these relationships tend to be unnecessarily complicated and confusing.

This can be seen in the reaction of a mother who becomes disproportionately emotional when her children leave to go to dad's house. It's as if she can't bear the thought of it. If her children feel responsible for her well-being, in response to an enmeshed relationship, they are likely to cry loudly, make a fuss, lash out and/or refuse to leave their mother behind. They may even shout, "I don't wanna go!" When people are entangled and seem unable to experience separate emotions, as a result, it's safe to say that their worlds are enmeshed.

Helicopter parenting is another example, as is any situation in which a parent becomes overly-involved in their children's lives or vice versa. In the stepfamily home, this dynamic is seen in daughters who act like "mini wives" to their fathers. Dads who don't put an end to this behavior perpetuate the problem. In fact, they help drive a wedge between their new wives and their daughters by failing to: Set, communicate and hold strong personal boundaries. Enmeshed, too, is the child of divorced parents who tries to protect one or both adults against feeling sad, hurt or disappointed. These children feel a deep need (or urge) to "step up" and protect their parents, though this is not an appropriate role for them. If anything, it delays their own development. It can also result in codependency which lingers into adulthood and negatively impacts the relationships they have with themselves and others.

If you witness any of these behaviors in your stepfamily, speak up. By that I mean have a candid but considerate conversation with your partner about what you're witnessing. As a stepparent coming into a somewhat ready-made family, you're often able to view behaviors and habits more objectively. That's because they're new to you and have long stopped being apparent or annoying to him. Without being judgmental, tell him what it is you're concerned about. There are any number of ways to start that conversation. A few ways you can do that are outlined below.

Use "I" statements, whenever possible, saying something like:

- I notice Ashlee seems to be protective of you. Is that new?
- I wonder: Is leaving Mom's house usually difficult for Archie?
- I think Bri is overly concerned about her mom. What do you think?
- When I see Max upset over his mom being alone, it worries me. How 'bout you?

Approach your spouse without crossing his own personal boundaries related to his children and their behaviors or mannerisms. This is why emphasizing "I" statements is important. Another thing to avoid is imposing your views on him or anyone else. As adults, we all have free will and need to be given the freedom to do what we think is best. This is particularly true when it comes to our children who, at the end of the day, are a parent's responsibility. If his views on these issues differ from yours, remain open-minded and explain that you're curious to know more about his perspectives. This will help you engender trust versus turn him off to the topic completely.

Being in a relationship—romantic or otherwise—isn't about getting everyone to think the same way; in fact, that tactic finds many stepfamilies struggling. It's about showing respect for our differences and learning to coexist despite them. You're never likely to view his relationships with his kids or his ex the way he does. Give him room to define and navigate them as he sees fit (based on his *own* values and beliefs) and you'll be one step closer to getting on the same page. If a related situation infringes on your personal space or conflicts with your personal values and beliefs, have a conversation about how you might remedy the situation either alone or with help from a qualified and experienced stepfamily professional.

Physical Boundaries

Physical boundaries include those which have an impact on our moods. For example, "Can I get a little privacy, please?" They also include those which have an impact on our bodies: "Uh, I really don't like to be tickled." We'll begin this discussion with insights into how creating space in which to think, do and be all impact the relationships we have with ourselves and our stepfamilies. We'll then discuss issues related to physical intimacy and interactions.

Believe it or not, as much as you love your partner, you need physical space to yourself. We all do. For me, it's as crucial as breathing. I need a place to call my own. That's the case whether Bernard and I are at home, traveling or holed up in our RV. I don't care whether it's a table, a bed to spread out on, a special section of the bathroom for "my" stuff or a clothes closet. It simply needs to be a place in which I can regroup and privately collect my thoughts. It's where I go to be alone and to spend time being "me." Take some time to explore what physical space means to you. Once you've defined it, promise yourself to honor and defend it. This is your own, private sanctuary we're talking about. This need is true for your spouse, too, so give him that courtesy. (Man cave, anyone?)

It's also true for your stepkids, whether they live with you full-time, part-time or only occasionally. All children need to know and feel as if they have a place in your home. That place should create and foster a sense of belonging in them. While growing up, my childhood bedroom was an area I found challenging. I had little personal or physical space to myself, making that room feel like anything but a safe place for me to retreat to. With that in mind, when my stepdaughters were teens, one of the boundaries we put in place was around what their rooms could be used for. They could eat whatever and whenever was reasonable, which we defined, except for in any of the bedrooms. We did this so as not to find food rotting under their beds or in their drawers. (We had, actually, on prior occasions.)

I realize some families don't take issue with this. My own husband was okay with them eating anywhere they liked until the day we started to notice a funny odor upstairs. It was at that moment he decided, yes, we should implement a no-food-in-your-rooms policy. Enforcing this new rule was difficult at first. There were lots of arguments over it. Finally, Bernard and I realized that we needed to put natural consequences in place: The offender was to pick up the rotting food, throw it away, hand wash related dishes with detergent and scrub the carpet or drawer until the smell was gone. It wasn't a pleasant task. In the end, the consequence got their attention and ensured their cooperation.

This is what setting clear and healthy boundaries looks like in action. The result is a home in which everyone feels safe and secure, knowing how they're to interact with one another and their shared environment. Once each member of your stepfamily knows what's expected of them and what's sure to happen when your boundaries are crossed, it's up to you to maintain them. Kids *will* test both you and your boundaries. So, how you choose to create and maintain a pleasant physical environment is an important conversation to have with your spouse. It's best done as you begin to build your stepfamily. But it's never too late! Start now, if you haven't done it already.

Physical space is also related to the very real distance that exists between you (or someone else in your stepfamily) and another person. Setting adequate and appropriate boundaries in this area requires each of you to consider what's okay and what's not okay. Do that in relation to the following and other activities, though you and your partner should likely have the biggest say in what you feel is safe and beneficial regarding the kids' well-being:

- *Kissing* – Are we talking cheeks? Lips?
- *Hugging* – What's too close for comfort?
- *Touching* – When does it become inappropriate?
- *Conversation* – What's the most comfortable distance?
- *Stepsibling interaction* – At what point does it cross the line?

Unless we're arguing with them, how close someone gets when they're talking to us or standing behind us in line at the grocery store sometimes amounts to personal preference. It can even have roots in cultural conditioning. I learned this while traveling in Europe and Asia. In both regions, people seem comfortable standing this|close|to one another. I, on the other hand, prefer a bit of distance—between myself and strangers. Take some time now to think about your own physical body. How far or wide does your own comfort zone ... *reach?*

Consider this in the context of sharing physical space with your partner, your stepkids, your own kids, your extended family and even pets. Then consider how it may change with regard to strangers. For each relationship, ask yourself when it is you begin to feel as if your physical safety zone is being encroached upon. For most people, arm's length conversations with acquaintances or strangers feels about right. That's because you're just close enough to engage in conversation and to connect. Any farther and you may find that it's hard to establish trust with the individual or that you're distracted by your surroundings. Any closer and you may feel as if your space has been invaded; you may even feel threatened, subconsciously or consciously.

This is especially true when engaged in an argument, during which physical space dictates whether you feel able to continue on or experience a sudden, desperate urge to walk away. Reflect back on the last argument you may have had with your spouse, your (step-)kids or the ex. Were you able to focus on the words being said or were you more worried about your physical safety? What was your gut feeling about proximity, whether you were standing too close to them or they were standing too close to you? In everyday conversations, as well, the presence or absence of physical space does a lot to influence how we feel.

Cultural anthropologist, educator and author Edward T. Hall, PhD, who coined the term "proxemics" and wrote *The Silent Language,* studied proximity and how it affects the way people communicate nonverbally with each other. Depending on your cultural origins and where you grew up, he found, your level of comfort in close quarters will vary. This can explain why, as a stepparent, you may feel uncomfortable cozying up to your stepkids or the ex.

Hall's work led to the identification of four distinct proximity spheres:

- Intimate, 6–18 in. (15–45 cm) – This physical distance hints at a closeness or comfort between individuals and is common when hugging, whispering or snuggling.

- Personal, 1.5-4 ft. (45-120 cm) – This physical distance is common among family members and close friends. Increased comfort and closeness often indicate greater intimacy.
- Social, 4-12 ft. (1.20-3.50 m) – This physical distance is common among acquaintances. The more frequently you interact, the more comfortable you'll be interacting closely.
- Public, 12-25 ft. (3.50-7.50 m) – This physical distance is common in settings where you may be addressing a group of strangers or giving a workplace presentation.

Think again about your stepfamily, this time as if it's a micro-community you recently moved into. It takes a while to get to know the people within that community. You may be the type of person who has an open-door policy, meaning you're comfortable with just about anyone coming and going in your home. There are others, like myself, who feel as if their whole homes are sanctuaries for them. If that describes you, rather than immediately being open to letting anyone in, you have a need to first become more familiar with them.

Knowing which scenario suits you and the individual members of your stepfamily will give you a better understanding of what personal and physical space mean to each of you. From there, you can start setting boundaries which take everyone's preferences and needs into account. Find common ground, if possible, and set rules which help demonstrate respect for, protect and preserve everyone's personal and physical comfort. Comfort, by the way, is key. You want to get to a place where you're comfortable in each other's presence. Expect your comfort levels to change over time, as your relationships grow more intimate.

Know this, too: When our comfort levels are tested by disagreements or disputes, it's common for us to grow less intimate with one another. Some people even shut themselves out behind real or imaginary walls, seeking protection against hurt feelings or perceived threats. If it's you who feels uncomfortable, it's okay to close your gate for a while and to survey the stepfamily landscape through the slats in your fence.

Just be mindful to avoid locking anyone out, permanently.

CHAPTER 8

Shared Bathrooms, Social Media & Sex

Setting boundaries within your stepfamily takes many forms. In this chapter, we'll cover a few special topics which benefit from upfront consideration by you and your partner. This should happen long before you begin discussing or, if you choose, negotiating them with any (step-)children who'll be affected by them. I'll cover, in detail: *Shared Bathrooms*, *Social Media* and *Sexual Behavior*. While it's common for most families to already have House Rules and/or boundaries in place regarding these issues, I encourage you to read on versus skip this section.

Like *Personal Boundaries* and *Physical Boundaries*, which we discussed in the last chapter, a lack of boundaries in these other three areas often incites confusion among my coaching practice clients. That's because many of them consider these topics taboo or anticipate them as being difficult to navigate. Who among us wants to openly discuss bathroom habits or sexual routines—with our kids, no less? Or face any backlash we may encounter, if and when we ask them to be considerate in their use of social media at home, while on vacation or elsewhere? Too few of us, I find.

Getting clear, as a couple, will minimize any disagreements you have over encouraging preferred behaviors in these three domains. Make time to learn about and discuss each one, arriving at a set of related rules which then safeguard the daily needs, privacy and safety of every member of your household. What works in my home or your neighbor's home may not work in yours. So, while you want to follow a few basic guidelines, be sure your own boundaries are informed by a value system which only you and your partner need to agree on.

Shared Bathrooms

Of the many spaces we share in our homes, bathrooms (as well as bedrooms) top the list of areas in which we all hope to get a little respite and can benefit from boundaries which ensure our privacy. The younger your children and stepchildren are, the more likely it is they'll either follow you into them or require help and guidance when using them. Once our children become adolescents and teens, their ability and desire to navigate them alone increases. I'll assume you're dealing with a mix of age ranges since, like me, you may also have (step-)grandkids.

Begin by asking yourselves a few questions:

- Does your stepfamily share one bathroom?
- If not, do you have a dedicated kids' bathroom?
- If there's a couple's bathroom, is it okay for kids to use it?
- If one person's showering, can another person use the toilet?
- If so, does that rule apply to same gender *and* mixed gender occupants?

On the surface, some of those questions might seem silly. Yet, if you haven't made time to discuss them already, talking about them now can save you a lot of heartache later on.

Other bathroom topics worth pondering:

- Is it OK for parents to shower/bathe with their children?
- If so, at what age does this habit seem inappropriate?
- Is it OK for the kids to shower or bathe together?
- If so, does that rule apply to a mix of genders?
- Again, at what age should that habit end?

This topic can be a sensitive one, since we all grew up under different circumstances. If you grew up with an open-door policy on bathroom sharing and your husband didn't, you may butt heads as you set some ground rules for your stepfamily bathroom(s). Think back to how heated the public debate around bathroom use in North Carolina became, when transgender students were forbidden from using bathrooms assigned to the genders they associated with versus the ones they were assigned at birth. For those students, that incited a mix of fear and anxiety. While this is an atypical example, it does emphasize how delicate the topic of sharing bathrooms can be.

Jean is a stepmom of two who once asked me what I thought about her fifteen-year-old stepson showering with his nine-year-old sister. She mentioned that the siblings had been taking showers together since they were little. She found this arrangement highly uncomfortable and asked her husband to put a stop to it. He didn't see anything wrong with this practice: It was something his kids had grown up doing and something he'd grown up doing, too. My personal opinion and response emphasized their age differences, though gender did play a role given they were moving through separate developmental stages. Despite what dad says or thinks, I find the practice inappropriate.

Parents, stepparents and other caregivers (i.e., babysitters, relatives) should focus on ensuring that each child's needs are met when it comes to: safety, well-being and age-appropriate activity. There's a caveat to this. Tolerating something you strongly disagree with, as a stepmom, is not the same as reaching a compromise. What's more, it can lead to serious and damaging physical or emotional consequences. Let's say these kids are three- and four-year-old stepsiblings. One is your daughter and the other is your stepson. What then? It's likely that, as they take that shower or bath, you or someone you trust is right there with the children. There's some form of adult supervision in place.

Still, for you and your partner to be okay with this, consider:

- The kids' comfort levels and relationships
- Your comfort level with nudity in the home
- Your individual views on nudity and the body
- Your values and beliefs around physical space
- Your values and beliefs around personal space

While there's no perfect answer, remember that the goal of setting boundaries within your stepfamily is to give each of you the space and freedom to express yourselves without endangering the others in any way. This doesn't mean everyone in your home needs to agree with every boundary you set. Still, the end goal of every decision you and your partner make is to ensure the safety, respect and dignity of every family member. Note, too, that if you allow one child to do certain things (i.e., you let your teen daughter use your bathroom to shave her legs in, since it has a large tub), you can expect that the others will want the same or similar privileges as a matter of fair treatment.

As children and stepchildren grow, your boundaries around bathroom use need to change and grow with them. Teens primp and preen in ways younger siblings rarely do. Your boundaries must be fluid enough to account for changes in grooming habits and lifestyle. It's normal to adjust boundaries as kids age and your family diminishes (or grows) in size. If what was first established as a boundary isn't working for everyone, do some reevaluating. Adjust and, if appropriate, renegotiate your bathroom boundaries. Consider differences in the children's genders, ages and greater/lesser need for privacy—with teens likely wanting or needing more of it. Consider your family home. Are there enough bathrooms to go around? If not, when an older sibling is showering in the kids' bathroom, can the younger children use yours? Would a kids' shower schedule or a 15-minute time limit help at all?

Once you and your partner have carefully thought these things through, have a Stepfamily Meeting and share your decisions with everyone else. Let them know that the bathroom boundaries you're putting in place are for everyone's benefit and are to be respected. If they play a role in carrying them out, tell them exactly what that is: "Junior, we want you to have enough time to get ready for your afterschool job. We just ask that you limit your shower time to 10 minutes, so your younger siblings won't have to wait so long to pee." (It's best to keep it real!)

Make a point of telling the children how the rules benefit them, as well as everyone else, since you want any boundaries you set to remain in place and to be respected whether you're there to enforce them or not. This is why, "Because I said so," is an ineffective comeback to any objections they might raise. Hear them out and see if you can make some concessions. If not, explain why. Otherwise, as soon as you head out the door, the kids will take advantage of your ambiguity and do whatever they like. In other words, they'll disrespect your wishes. This is true whether you're setting boundaries around bathroom use or anything else.

Do you already have boundaries in place which aren't being abided by? I wouldn't be surprised, though it's never too late to have a sit down and figure out why. Are the kids calling the other parent to complain that they "can't use the bathroom in peace," feel like they're "not welcome" in your home or have to follow a bunch of "stupid bathroom rules" they don't agree with? This is where circling back to your couple's *why* and how it ties in with your values and beliefs is important. Boundaries aren't a form of punishment. They're a tool for getting everyone's needs met. As best you can, calmly and patiently initiate a bathroom boundaries conversation.

Maybe you've declared your couple's bathroom off-limits to everyone else. Hey, that's your prerogative! Kids can be messy. On top of that, in order to get to your bathroom, they may need to go through your bedroom or other highly personal space. (I know I'm uncomfortable having other people marching through my bedroom at all hours.) You may even be afraid that they'll either root through your things or break something. These are valid concerns, so don't apologize for your own need for privacy. You and your partner, as adults, have earned that privilege. By setting bathroom boundaries thoughtfully, you ensure everyone's privacy. That includes your own.

Social Media

These days, nearly everyone's posting photos and real-time updates online. There are the pictures from last year's trip to Disneyland. The pictures you took on the beach. The pictures from that long-awaited family reunion. The pictures from one or more of the kids' birthday parties. Holiday get-togethers, girlfriend gatherings, couple's night out—it's all there. We love sharing these events and experiences with extended family, friends living in far flung places and anyone else we follow or allow to follow us on social media.

Yet, social media is a big issue when it comes to setting and maintaining boundaries. The use of platforms such as Facebook, Twitter, Instagram and Snapchat—to name just a few—can contribute to or incite stepfamily conflict in a number of ways. It's practically second nature for us to share too much, share what's going on in the privacy of our own homes and share stuff that's not meant for others' prying eyes. We may even air our grievances online.

What happens, though, when your stepdaughter complains about how terribly "her stepmom" (aka you) treats her? Never mind that the root cause of her rant was you not allowing her to stay out after midnight, which she knows is well past her curfew. She won't mention that. And what about that cute picture you shared of your stepson at the birthday party you threw for him? Was it really okay for you to post that publicly? Questions such as these highlight concerns about the widespread use of social media and the appropriateness of *what* and with *whom* we share online.

Having honest, open stepfamily conversations about social media and internet use is extremely important. Privacy and security issues are crucial to pay attention to, as one click can land us and our family members who knows where. So, make setting firm and clear boundaries around social media use in your home a real topic of concern. If we lived in a perfect world—where all parents came together to raise kids and followed the same guidelines for what's "in the kids' best interests"—we wouldn't have to worry. Alas, this isn't the case. You must put boundaries in place.

When it comes to social media, ask yourselves:

- Where do we draw the line—online?
- What's okay to post, as a (step-)child?
- What's okay to post, as a (step-)parent?
- How much is too much social media time?
- Who is it okay to friend or follow on social media?

Studies into the effects of prolonged and continuous use of smartphones and video games show that *both* impair our ability to socialize with people close to us. If you see your children and/or stepchildren every other weekend or sporadically over the course of a year, social media and related apps might seem like an ideal way to keep in contact with them. With little effort or engagement, you can get a peek at what's happening in their worlds. Doing so may even give you a sense that you know what's going on. In reality, though, what we see on social media may *not* be representative of any of it. After all, what you see posted is what the other person chooses for you to see.

In the article "Social Media Use and Social Connectedness in Adolescents: The Positives and the Potential Pitfall," a team of four Australia-based academics shared their insights into how social media use impacts our children's development—as it relates to their sense of belonging, psychological well-being and identity formation—and how it impacts their growth processes. Through their research, Kelly A. Allen, PhD, Tracii Ryan, PhD, DeLeon L. Gray, PhD, and Dennis M. McInerney, PhD, found that "online tools create a paradox for social connectedness." While they can increase the ease with which we form, join and maintain relationships (or communities) online, these four researchers found that they can also be "a source of alienation and ostracism."

Related U.S.-based research, conducted for The Pew Charitable Trusts, shows that 81 percent of teens with internet access use Facebook to forge their identities and to stay connected with friends. Both of those tasks are age-appropriate, by the way. Facebook then allows those teens to "meet" others with similar interests, share their personal experiences and create a sense of identity for themselves. The dangers lie in our (step-)children's subsequent exposure to cyberbullying, sexual harassment and cyberostracism. Allen, Ryan, Gray and McInerney have backed this up, noting that teens who frequently turn to social media experience higher rates of loneliness and feel more disconnected, overall, than teens who engage in a greater number of face-to-face relationships.

Yet, what about you? While on social media, have you ever been stalked or bullied by the ex? Has she made a public show of blaming you for how awful her life is now that you're with her former partner? Maybe she gloats about how much better her life is now that she's "over him" and he's "your responsibility." She may even make a point of posting critical comments anytime you share pictures of yourself which include "her children" or her former spouse. She can, if your page isn't set to private or if you accepted her Friend Request to avoid causing any friction.

While I hate to say it, for all I know, you may have retaliated by publicly or anonymously badmouthing her online. My point is, when it comes to social media and technology, it's likely that your entire family will benefit by setting stronger boundaries around their usage. In a report for "20/20" (the results of which aired in May 2017), Elizabeth Vargas investigated the habits of three separate families whose members had become addicted to technology. The effects of their obsessions, she found, were felt across each of their family structures.

Say you notice that your teen stepdaughter has stopped interacting with those she physically shares space with, opting to stare intently into her phone over dinner. Or that your stepson spends most of his time in his room, texting with everyone from close friends to complete strangers. Either way it's time for an intervention. Those kids may even anticipate a talking to. A 2018 Pew Research Center study showed that 50 percent of teens believe they "spend too much time" on their smartphones and have started policing their *own* use of such devices. Other studies show that 60 to 65 percent of parents are concerned about their children's smartphone addictions and have begun setting "screen-time restrictions" within their homes. Device manufacturers themselves have begun developing products, such as Apple iOS 12, aimed at helping those who love their phones "a little too much" cut back on their usage.

Why all the hubbub? Well, the more we're online the more prone we are to being tracked or stalked while using our computers and cell phones. You or another member of your stepfamily may already be experiencing this. The good news is, aside from minimizing time spent online, there are ways to fix the problem. First? Un-friend, un-follow or otherwise undo your connection to the offending organization or individual. Second, change your social media privacy settings. As an added measure, block unwanted persons from gaining access to you.

I regularly review the list of people who've followed me on social media. If there's any doubt as to their legitimacy or motives, I block them. This is a firm boundary I've set to protect myself and those in my social circle. Being "social" should never be reason enough to risk your own safety and security or that of your stepfamily members—especially when there are relatively simple measures you can take to put an end to it. Start cleaning house on the social media front by first outlining the reasons online interaction is a *benefit* to you.

Social media benefits, for your stepfamily, might include:

- It helps Dad stay connected to his kids.
- It lets the kids share their successes with him.
- It lets you introduce one another to family/friends.
- It helps you stay connected to out-of-town family/friends.
- It lets you quickly say, "Hey!" and check in with each other.

After doing that, determine who it is and isn't okay to interact with. Next, decide when and where you and your family members will use social media. Some stepfamilies set firm boundaries around dinnertime and Stepfamily Night, banning the use of all forms of technology for set periods of time. If you choose this route, be sure that you and your partner also adhere to such guidelines. If there are times you're unable to, because you're waiting for a business call, be sure to say so upfront. Finally, as a stepfamily, discuss what's okay to post online and what's not.

One of my stepdaughters asked us to *not* post photos of her children online. She explained herself, saying that she wouldn't be posting any either. She let us know that she was happy to share photos with us back and forth via text, email or some other, alternative method. We respected her wishes for anonymity on social platforms and, while it's no longer through social media, still get to share in what's happening with our grandkids living far away.

Other technology-related steps you can take:

- Consider banning cell phones in bedrooms.
- Set up a central stepfamily computer station.
- With your spouse, set limits around phone use.
- With your spouse, set limits for social media use.
- Use apps to monitor household phone and data use.

These are simply suggestions, since what works for one stepfamily won't work for another. Any number of variables can also make enforcing some of these rules or limits a challenge. Let's say that, as a stepmom, you're upset that your stepdaughter often ignores your texts. Her response might be that she doesn't keep her phone nearby. You know, however, that if she fails to quickly respond to her mom's texts her phone gets taken away from her for an entire week. When you mention this, she replies, "Well, *you're* not the one paying my cell phone bill. Mom is."

Dad, who's sitting nearby, doesn't say a word to either of you. You're now clearly upset by your stepdaughter's response and believe she's being disrespectful. Your stepdaughter, caught in a loyalty bind, is also upset and feels a need to defend her mother/daughter relationship. Dad doesn't want to get caught in the middle of this argument. Still, as your stepdaughter turns to leave, you ask him, "Are you going to let her get away with this?" No reply.

Here's the deal: In this scenario, there's a lot going on behind the scenes. One, you're upset by your stepdaughter's nonchalance about replying to your texts. Two, you may have an uncommunicated expectation that she reply within a certain timeframe. Three, mom and daughter have their own set of rules in place—which may conflict with your expectations for your stepdaughter. Dad may have *not* wanted his daughter to have a cell phone at all. Now that she has one, he may not have set any requirements for its use except to say that she's not allowed to use it at mealtime.

None of you are operating from the same guidelines. You and her dad aren't even on the same page. Boundaries around phone use, in your home, are clearly missing or haven't been communicated. You can't dictate what goes on in the other home, so don't even try. (It's not your place to, anyhow.) A better approach is to say, "I feel like I'm being ignored when I text you and don't get a response. Worse, I start to worry about your safety." That's the real issue here or should be. While you feel as if you're being ignored, you then begin to worry about your stepdaughter's whereabouts. Still, teens hate to be monitored constantly. Yes, some kids do require tighter surveillance. Others? Not so much. Base related decisions on individual children's capabilities and prior outcomes.

This is where Dad needs to step in, initiating a conversation with his kids about responding to his and your texts or phone calls. If your stepkids don't feel comfortable texting you directly, he can suggest that you communicate using a group text feature which includes him in the conversation. Whatever your solution, be sure it's age-appropriate and gives his children the room they need to grow, learn and individuate responsibly.

Discuss the details of this privately before approaching them, so that neither you nor your partner is positioned to be the middle man or the bad guy. Get clear about your own expectations, have your partner share his and reach an agreement you can both live with. Then communicate your household's boundaries around social media and/or cell phone use to the children. Be willing to listen to their concerns but do what you two feel is best. As needed or desired, post your related House Rules on either the fridge door or their bedroom doors. And always lead by example, since modeling the behaviors you want to see demonstrated is a must. This is particularly important when you're asking them to carry out new rules and adapt to new boundaries, though it will always benefit you to do so.

Sexual Behavior

I'd like to share an important note about sexual boundaries in stepfamilies: There's *never* a time when intimate relationships between stepchildren and stepparents or between stepsiblings is appropriate. These types of boundaries need to be clearly defined and communicated at the onset of any such relationships. For some, it may seem obvious or even ridiculous to have these conversations. Yet, children continue to be cornered by and sometimes molested by close family members, distant relatives and family friends. Rare is a molester or rapist a stranger, especially when this activity takes place in the children's homes. Tips for approaching this topic with your partner follow.

It's not unusual to avoid sensitive or delicate topics out of embarrassment or for fear that we'll seem insensitive or be thought of as insinuating that our partners or their children might be capable of such behaviors. One way to address this issue and to start a dialogue around it is to say, "John, there's something I'd like to discuss with you. It concerns our need to establish boundaries around sexual behavior for the kids' sake. Will you talk with me about this?" If the timing isn't quite right, decide on a time that works well for both of you but don't keep putting it off.

If your partner refuses to have this conversation, you might say: "John, I sense that even the thought of having this conversation is making you uncomfortable. Is there a particular reason you don't want to talk about it?" Take time to listen to and validate his own concerns. Then let him know why you feel this is something you have to make time for. Offer to set a timer for 20 or 30 minutes, letting him know that you just want to express your concerns and hear his views on the subject. As a result, you'll be able to establish clear and firm boundaries which apply to everyone.

Once you're in agreement, have a serious conversation about how you can help protect all of your children against harm. Depending on the kids' ages, this may even be a good time to get clear about your shared views on sex and intimacy. (Pretending they don't think about or won't be affected by these things is simply naïve.) Doing this will help you put guidelines in place for other topics of an intimate and sexual nature—ones you can then communicate to your kids either one-on-one or in a Stepfamily Meeting.

Sex-related topics worth discussing with the kids:

- Birth control
- Premarital sex/intimacy
- Sexual maturity and activity
- Intimacy and your shared home
- Boyfriend/girlfriend relationships

Conversations about dress code should also be included. Is it okay to walk around your home naked, in low-cut tops or in extremely short shorts? Is it okay for the kids to cuddle up in bed, or co-sleep, with you and your partner? If so, at what age does it become *not* okay? As needed, reiterate your family's policies on bathroom behavior: showering, bathing, etc. The list of issues you can address, when it comes to talking about sex and intimacy, could go on and on.

A great way to start is by creating your own list and then sharing it with your partner. You'll need to revisit these topics at different points in your stepfamily relationship, as the kids: grow older, begin dating, transition to living with you full-time, take more overnight trips, etc. Whatever the timing, don't neglect this conversation until it becomes a matter of major importance.

Talking about sex now will save you headaches, heartaches and heated debates down the road.

CHAPTER 9

How to Set Healthy Boundaries

The work we've done so far was intended to help you: Define boundaries, consider why they're important, clarify a few of your own and work with your partner to address the sorts of behaviors which impact your stepfamily home on a daily or ongoing basis. Now it's time to start setting healthy boundaries in other areas of your lives; ones which may also impact your day-to-day routine but are more likely to affect how your stepfamily functions long-term.

In particular, we'll talk about boundaries related to:

- Word choice
- Emotional safety
- Financial security
- Religion/spirituality

The words we use when communicating with one another, the emotions we trigger in others, our sense of financial obligation and our right to religious or spiritual freedom are all topics you and your partner need to address at some point. Before digging into each one, I'd like to remind you that demonstrating respect for the boundaries within your stepfamily home is a two-way street. The children or stepchildren who live in your household look to you and your partner for guidance and modeling when it comes to respecting any boundaries you've set.

Rather than simply talk the talk, you have to walk the walk—just as you hope they'll do. This means keeping your word, honoring your promises and following through with associated consequences. It's up to you, as a couple, to model how your household boundaries are to be carried out. If you do what you say, there's a good chance the kids will do the same. If they don't live with you full-time or are asked to follow a different set of rules in their other parents' homes, make a pact to let go of a need to control what goes on when they're not with you. This can be a real test of your nerves but it's totally doable.

When your (step-)children are out with friends or are sleeping over at their friends' homes, you have no control over what it is they do there. So, if you have to, think of the other household that way. More importantly, when they are with you, it's more effective to show them what responsible behavior looks like than to tell them. Consistency is important, as well. So is being willing to say, "No," sometimes. Divorced parents often have a bit of difficulty with this, wanting to spare their children any further upset, yet you can make this easier on yourselves.

Follow up with a reason, giving them a clear understanding of why you object to a particular suggestion or activity. In the process, you'll be teaching them to think critically and to make wise decisions based on facts versus whims or desires. A truly poor excuse for not allowing them to do something is, "As long as you live in *this* house, you'll follow *our* rules." It not only reeks of dictatorship; it also robs them of the chance to understand how healthy decisions are made and the opportunity to make healthy decisions on their own. Whenever my parents said that, I felt unheard, disrespected and eager to leave home. It wasn't encouraging or nurturing. Still, I've caught myself saying the same exact thing to our kids only to regret it later. (I knew full well that it was the lamest excuse ever.)

Setting healthy boundaries requires equal doses of love/affection, trust and concern for ourselves, our partners and any children who are in our care. Boundaries which are arrived at with those things in mind are infinitely easier to enforce, too, since the feelings your family members then associate with them are *positive*. In addition, they foster greater respect for you and any House Rules you put in place. Conversely, when boundaries are created with a goal of wielding power over the other members of your household, the negativity embedded in them is palpable and is likely to incite fear, tension and stress.

The reason you want to set healthy boundaries, in the first place, is to ensure the children's health and safety. Yet, the same holds true for you and your spouse. When we set healthy boundaries for ourselves, it's to keep us safe so that we can continue making informed decisions which are healthful and in everyone's best interests. Boundaries aren't a series of, "No," responses. In fact, healthy boundaries help us confidently say, "Yes!" and feel good about it.

When it comes to stepchildren (or, for that matter, any children under our care), the key to setting healthy boundaries is keeping in mind what's age-appropriate. For example, let's say your eleven-year-old stepdaughter wants to take part in a sleepover. If neither you nor your partner have met the parents hosting this get together and have no way of meeting them prior to, ask yourselves if it's a good idea. Do your due diligence and arrive at answers to a few basic questions. The first thing you'll both want to know is who'll be supervising the sleepover.

Beyond that, it's important to ask your kids (or yourselves):

- What's the address and phone number?
- What are the other children's age ranges?
- Will the kids be home all night or going out?
- Is a party involved which includes the opposite sex?
- Do you expect there to be drinking, smoking or drug use?

Safety is paramount. Don't be swayed by tearful pleas about not trusting your stepdaughter. Though, if she's misbehaved in the past, it may be harder for you and your partner to believe that it's a good idea for her to participate. In that case, maybe she needs to actively work to regain your trust before a sleepover can be approved. Tell her exactly that without endlessly rehashing prior transgressions. Ultimately, the questions you ask should be the same ones you'd want her to ask herself before jumping into a potentially unsafe or unsupervised situation.

Some stepparents tell me, "Well, I did those things when I was her age—and I turned out okay!" Today's kids are exposed to lots more than we were at their ages. The amount of information and misinformation they can glean from the internet, social media and one another is confusing and can impair their ability to make good judgment calls. The role of a parent is to help them make sense of it all. Be upfront with them about where you're coming from, making a clear distinction between issues of trust and concerns over appropriateness.

Tell them you're willing to let them do certain things at the appropriate time versus saying, "No," out of a lack of trust. You'll gain greater trust in them, in fact, by being allowed to guide them in ways which sync up with your stepfamily's values and beliefs. You and your partner aren't there to be the kids' friends; biological or otherwise, you're there to parent them. You're on their side and willing to provide the support needed to ensure they grow into responsible adults. Boundaries ensure that the environment they grow up in is safe and secure, preparing them to independently say, "No," to peer pressure and develop healthy relationships of their own.

Let's tackle one last subject related to trust before moving on. If you're a stepmom who's still in the early stages of stepfamily life, know that a certain level of trust must be established before any boundaries you set will be effective. Your partner can move this process along, by making it known that he trusts your judgment and that you have his full support in making decisions regarding his children when he's unavailable to do so, such as when he's out of town or working late: You are *not* to be disrespected and the children are *not* to talk back to you.

We stepparents are often viewed as and can feel like "outsiders" in our own homes. We're thought of as disrupting "the way things used to be" or have been done for a very long time. It's even possible that the children and their other parent(s) are bent on creating boundaries designed to protect the sanctity of what used to be "their" family together. This makes it even more important that your partner communicates clearly what it is he expects of his children when it comes to abiding by any new boundaries and rules the two of you put in place for them.

To foster a greater sense of trust in your stepfamily home, when it comes to particular sets of desired behaviors or chores, narrow down who's responsible for overseeing what. Determine what it is your husband will be responsible for, what it is you'll be responsible for and what it is the kids will be responsible for. Then, set household boundaries which reflect that division of responsibility. Finally, communicate this to the children.

The benefits of sharing the burden include:

- Greater respect for House Rules
- Increased calm and harmony
- Higher self-esteem levels
- Greater accountability
- A sense of reliability

By taking a clear and logical approach to setting and enforcing boundaries, you teach the children to set their own boundaries and to value their own contributions to the household. Everyone will know who's responsible for what. By sharing ownership of those boundaries with everyone in your stepfamily, you give everyone the chance to act responsibly and to gain the rewards associated with it: increased trust, independence and interdependence. When a problem or disagreement arises, you'll all be better equipped to calmly arrive at a solution that works for everyone. Under these conditions, any rift over boundaries will be readily apparent.

If and when an issue arises, you can then:

- Identify which boundary was compromised.
- Discuss what makes this rule a family priority.
- Review the guidelines you already have in place.
- Revise those guidelines, as needed, going forward.
- Solve the problem assertively rather than aggressively.

None of this means that you or your spouse should expect to run a household that's devoid of disrespect or is free of lapses in cooperation. That'd be as unrealistic for your stepfamily as it is for first families. What you can expect—as you set boundaries which take love/affection, trust and concern for everyone in your home into consideration—is a sense of relief. You'll know that you did everything you could to lay a foundation for healthy behaviors. You'll also have an easier time setting, negotiating and enforcing boundaries the two of you believe make sense for your kids.

Word Choice

The saying, "Sticks and stones may break my bones but words will never hurt me," implies that we can say whatever we want to someone else. Well, that simply isn't true. Words are extremely powerful: They can uplift us or bring us crashing down. The words we use, as we interact with others, do have an impact. An epidemic of bullying has sprung up right alongside social media, with people now using words to knock others around at will. In some cases, the recipients of those attacks even contemplate suicide. If words aren't impactful, why is that so?

Children adopt language patterns they learn in the home. This is why we need to set firm boundaries around the words we use and how we use them. Speaking half-truths fosters a belief that's it okay to lie. Using (or ignoring the use of) profanity in the home encourages children to cuss in other settings. Making assumptions, well, that has the power to "make an ass out of you and me." If you make it known that you suspect your husband's ex is out to get you, can you back it up with facts? Even if you can, is that something your stepchildren should hear about?

Strive, instead, to create a stepfamily culture that values and rewards honesty, dignity, restraint and fact-based communication. Encourage open dialogue which squelches a need or desire to fib. Talk as if the children are within earshot at every moment, since it's likely they are. No matter who brings disparaging news into your home about your stepkids or the ex—even if it's her own children—be the bigger person. Don't tolerate negativity and gossip. Gossiping, in and of itself, crosses a very real boundary. If it's not yours to share or speculate about, don't.

The topic of word choice again raises the issue of sharing too much. Set and hold fast to boundaries around sharing information about your spouse, stepchildren and stepfamily life with others. If you're having a disagreement, discuss it directly with the person involved (whether that's your husband, your stepson, your own son or the ex). If you're compelled to divulge the details of your life to someone outside of your stepfamily circle, stop. Then ask yourself: Why? Is it relevant to them? Am I trying to sway them to my side? Am I doing it to push someone else away?

If you're on the receiving end, ask yourself if you feel comfortable being in this position or have a need to know what it is the person is sharing. If not, ask *them* to stop. While you're at it, recognize that this is like putting children in a position of relaying messages from one home to the other. More often than not, those messages should come directly from you or your spouse and aren't appropriate for the children to know about. Instead, relay them in person or by phone. Better yet, by email—so you have a record of what was said and how the other household responded.

Emotional Safety

Most of us are comfortable dealing with emotions like happiness, joy, contentment and maybe even sadness or grief. As adults, by now life has taught us what to do in circumstances like those. Yet, learning to navigate a full range of emotions is part of the human experience. The kids in your home need to learn how to do it, too. In *This Book Has Feelings: Adventures in Instinct and Emotion*, Neil Scott, PhD, and Sandi Mann, PhD, suggest: "Emotion isn't always the result of noticing physical changes in our body and giving (them) emotional labels. Quite often, an emotion is the consequence of the way we interpret or explain the world around us. This explains why the same thing can happen to two people who then experience two totally different emotions as a consequence."

The way we process things affects how we proceed. One feature of a healthy sense of self is understanding and knowing how to work within our emotional boundaries. Put another way, it's directly impacted by our ability to develop a sense of recognition that helps us identify what we're feeling and then cope with our circumstances. Consider this a subclass of the *Personal Boundaries* we discussed earlier, through which we set limits to protect ourselves against being manipulated by or becoming enmeshed with emotionally-needy people.

Stepchildren often experience this when dealing with bereft parents who have difficulty accepting their divorces. At any time, but particularly during their early stages of development, it's emotionally unhealthy for children to be subjected to this sort of behavior. If it's happening to your stepchild, talk this over with your partner. Consider seeking professional counsel for him or her, helping them learn to set appropriate emotional boundaries. Be sure that whomever you choose understands stepfamily dynamics well and is skilled at working with children of divorce.

When you consider the role emotions play in your stepfamily home, know that it's up to each of us to take ownership of our feelings, attitudes and behaviors. This isn't the same as being able to control them or to stop ourselves from feeling them. It's a matter of being accountable. Every member of your household will benefit from learning—via the words, actions and interactions shared between you and your partner—to take ownership of their emotions and to reasonably regulate their reactions to them, as well as any knee-jerk responses they might trigger. Make time to deliberately sit down with your spouse and the children in your home, letting everyone know that they're responsible for understanding, respectfully managing and communicating their own perspectives.

Be sure to cover topics such as individual:

- Attitudes/Beliefs
- Feelings/Emotions
- Thoughts and Words
- Choices and/or Decisions
- Responses and/or Reactions

On the flipside, once they know this and begin to master those domains, the children will also benefit from being able to take greater personal responsibility for and subsequent pride in their ability to choose and apply their own:

- Personal Values
- Individual Talents
- Decision-Making Skills
- Limit-Setting Capabilities
- Hobbies, Passions or Desires

THE STEPMOM'S BOOK OF BOUNDARIES

Yet, what about emotions which—on their surface, at least—appear to conflict with your stepfamily's boundaries? Anger is one such emotion. Guidelines around expressions of anger in the home often appear to be blurry. Are you capable of allowing another member of your home to express his or her anger? If so, to what extent? Anger itself is neither good nor bad. It's in how we react to anger that we begin to view it as good or bad, healthy or unhealthy. When it's directed at improving our lives and relationships, anger can be viewed as a positive emotion.

Anger typically sets in when we perceive that an injustice has been done to us or to those we love/care about. We can also become angry over matters of social injustice. Anger is what motivates us to take action, hoping to right perceived wrongs. If your spouse is repeatedly denied access to his children for no other reason than his ex simply won't make time to arrange those visits or keeps changing the schedule at the last minute, anger is what motivates you to seek legal counsel, related advice and/or the help of a stepfamily coach or counselor.

What's unacceptable is a physically threatening or harsh verbal response to angry feelings. This behavior crosses very real boundaries related to personal safety and emotional security on the part of everyone involved. Yet, when directed properly, anger can be the driving force behind positive change. Consider the last time you felt angry. At the onset, were you able to think rationally? For most of us, the answer is a resounding, "No!" Stepfamily life presents us with lots of maddening situations. I suggest preparing yourself, in advance, to face angry feelings.

Learn to do that by practicing this exercise:

- When you're ready to scream, stop.
- Decide to take a Time-Out by yourself.
- Use that time to think things over carefully.
- Forget how "unfair" it all is and simply reflect.
- Note—or write down—what it is you're angry about.

It's only *after* you've taken these five simple steps that you can begin to communicate your upset to someone else. Getting to the root of why you're truly angry is key. Do you feel as if the ex is interfering with your or your partner's ability to see the kids? Are you angry because your stepkids continue to disrespect you, taking your things without asking or lying to others about what's really going on in your home? Do you feel as if your spouse takes you for granted? Could it be you feel angry at yourself for doing too much? Dig deep before reacting to your angry feelings and you just may find that they've been triggered by more than one event or situation.

Once you've had time to relax and reflect, ask yourself:

- Do I have all of the facts I need?
- If not, is there a way to gather them?
- Is there another explanation for all of this?
- What can be done to improve this situation?
- Is my inability to say, "No," part of the problem?

Clinical Psychologist Harriet Lerner, PhD, talks about our widespread challenges with anger in her bestselling book *The Dance of Anger*. For years, she states, anger was viewed as a societal ill; as an evil, inappropriate emotion which needed to be suppressed. When the same sorts of behaviors or circumstances repeatedly make us angry, she adds, there's usually a reason that's either been buried over or has been left unresolved. Failing to stand up for ourselves in these situations and to say, "No," or "That's not okay with me," can be one such culprit.

I remember my very first argument with Bernard. My husband and I were arguing over something the kids had done, which I had reacted to. I'm not quite sure anymore just what that was but, in my mind, I thought the whole blowup wasn't that big a deal. Bernard, however, felt as if I had crossed the line with his children. He held the belief that arguments are inherently bad and that our relationship had reached its end point. I was shocked to say the least.

Clearly, we got past it. Yet, there's more to the story. In my family of origin, it was common for everyone to both argue and talk loudly. None of us took the time to listen to what the other person was saying or to ask clarifying questions. This was our way of letting off steam. Although this method is highly unproductive, never did I imagine that it would precipitate the end of a relationship. For me, it was a learned method of venting before moving on.

After getting over my shock at having crossed a boundary that was new to me, Bernard and I sat down together. We processed our feelings and discussed ways our entire stepfamily could better argue and manage our anger. It took many attempts to get to a place in which we both felt heard and respected. Our boundaries around anger were a work in-progress, bringing us both as close to the edge of our respective fences as humanly possible. Now? We follow hard rules which are non-negotiable: In our home, there will never be hitting, name calling or degrading insults of any kind. Yet, we needed to approach the edge to establish emotional boundaries which truly work for us.

Financial Security

One area of life which can also incite arguments among stepfamily couples is finances. When it comes to money, some dads feel as if they "owe" their kids a great experience due to all of the time they miss out on with them. This can make your spouse or partner appear to be free with his money, especially—if not exclusively—when it comes to spending on his children. If you're the one handling the stepfamily finances, this sort of loosey-goosey approach can really begin to irk you. If not, you may still become fearful about your own financial security and future.

Whatever your situation, you must make time to sit together and discuss what you believe would be a healthy approach to managing and spending your household funds. As you do this, it's a good idea to consult an accountant, bookkeeper and/or expert financial planner who understands stepfamily dynamics. Things worth deciding, in advance, include how much you can comfortably budget (on a monthly or yearly basis) to account for each child's needs, activities, education, growth, etc.

At each stage of the stepfamily life cycle, major considerations include how much you agree to spend and who'll pay for what: you, your partner, the kids' other parents and/or their grandparents. When children are young, stepcouple conversations about money usually revolve around child support, child care expenses and alimony. When they become teenagers, talk then turns to cars, college and related expenses (i.e., gas, books, spending money). When they leave home, you're more likely to negotiate over expenses related to your children's weddings, entertaining the grandchildren and other things.

To the extent that you can, encourage your partner to also discuss these topics with his ex. If applicable, do the same with yours. Prior planning around child-related expenses will minimize tension within your home and between homes. Take into account each of the children's activities, school supply lists, clothing requirements, etc. A clear distinction needs to be made around each household's contributions to these items, especially if they're "nice to have" rather than necessary. Based on my professional experience, I've found that it's best to set these agreements in writing with the help of a lawyer or a skilled stepfamily mediator.

Another area of finance worth setting boundaries around is gift giving, including monetary gifts and/or loaning the children money. What's okay? What's not okay?

Do you and your partner feel there should be a household cap on the value of birthday, graduation or wedding gifts? Should you strive to spend an equal amount on each child? Holidays, birthdays and other special occasions can usually be anticipated, so plan accordingly. You could even set up one savings account for each of your children, teaching them to manage gifts of money or letting them use those funds to purchase gifts for others.

Some stepmothers maintain separate bank accounts of their own, which they individually withdraw from when they want to finance solo trips with their girlfriends, gifts for extended family members, personal indulgences (like that $300 designer purse you've been eyeing) and monthly salon or nail appointments. If you're in a position to keep an account that's separate, doing so will likely give you the added freedom and financial security to *not* feel guilty about spending a little bit on yourself now and then—or on other people who are important to you.

Finally, consider your last will and wishes. As much as we don't like to dwell on our mortality, growing old is a fact of life for all of us. One day, we'll die and our belongings will go somewhere. But where? With a will in place, you get to decide that upfront. Whether we're talking about cash, insurance payouts, stocks, real estate or other property and belongings, don't leave it for a court or anyone else to decide what happens to your assets. I'm not a financial planner or advisor, but I do suggest that you find and hire one who's worked with stepfamilies before.

My and Bernard's own philosophy around money is to be financially responsible now, planning for retirement and paying down our mortgage so that we won't become a burden to one another (or to our children) as we age. Being responsible with our money helped us greatly when it came to financing our kids' college educations, weddings and gifts for our grandkids. It also eased any guilty we may have otherwise felt when we later chose to reduce our level of spending on others and enjoy our empty-nest time together by traveling or going out more.

Religion/Spirituality

Not unlike politics, religion and spirituality can ignite some of the most heated debates. They can even cause new issues to spring up between family members and spouses. When we talk about faith, we're talking about your core beliefs. It's likely you've held onto these since childhood and you're entitled to them. Yet, as we grow, we sometimes begin to question them or wonder if another set of beliefs might better help us meet our individual needs.

Just as your parents instilled in you a set of core beliefs and values, your husband's parents did the same for him. When they were still together, he and his ex likely did the same for their own children. So, the range of beliefs and values you're grappling with now, as a stepmom, are broader still. How do you reconcile those differences? This is an area in which some people feel they have a right to tell you what you should and shouldn't believe.

But what happens when you're of one faith and your partner is of another? Or you take the kids to one sort of church service and the other household takes them to an entirely different kind? Shoving our religious or spiritual beliefs down other people's throats isn't only bad form; it crosses a clear religious and spiritual boundary. (When it happens to me, I don't like it one bit.) Can you live with the fact that your stepkids are of a different faith than you are? If you married their father, I would guess this is something you came to terms with before you both said, "I do."

If not, it's nobody else's fault but yours and his. So, make a point of respecting your differences. If your beliefs and your husband's are in opposition to one another, try to see each other's points of view as being just that. No one said you had to agree on everything. The best agreement you can make, in fact, is to allow yourselves to disagree without being bitter. Similarly, if your husband insists on trying to convert you to his religion, kindly let him know that you have no intention of switching. So, he may as well stop trying. Set a boundary, stick to it and move on.

Put an end to any attempts to bring one another over to the other person's side of the fence—whether it's yours, your partner's, your stepchildren's, the grandparents' or the exes.' Unless there's cult worship involved, focus on what you enjoy most about your chosen religious or spiritual practice and respectfully agree to disagree. By respecting one another's choices in faith (or lack thereof), you'll all experience fewer arguments and less stress.

In the next few chapters, we'll begin outlining ways you can tackle other areas which are prone to incite conflict in stepfamily relationships. They include, but are not limited to, the following topics—which stepmoms often contact me about when they reach out for help via my coaching practice:

- Manners, courtesy and respect
- Solitude, socializing and stepfamily time
- Household chores, maintenance and décor
- Health, hygiene, dress codes and appearance

- Co-parenting, parallel parenting, pick-up/drop-off
- Holiday, vacation and other time (i.e., work, play, rest)

I'll also share insights, tips and worksheets for setting boundaries in these areas and others.

CHAPTER 10

Stepfamily Boundaries—Why, When & How

As promised, in the previous chapter, this is where we'll begin putting healthy stepfamily boundaries in place. Before we do that, it's wise to consider what would happen if there were *no* boundaries or House Rules guiding the activity and behavior in your stepfamily home. Since you're reading this, I think it's safe to assume that your household currently suffers from a lack of boundaries or only has unofficial House Rules in place. Yet, would you like to know for sure? If so, I have an exercise for you. (Note: It's best to complete this with your partner.)

Ask yourselves a few questions:

- Do you argue over unspoken rules?
- Does anyone in your home feel powerless?
- Does anyone in your home experience anxiety?
- Does anyone in your home seem to be confused?
- Does anyone in your home hold unrealistic expectations?

Failing to put stepfamily boundaries or House Rules in place is the same as saying nothing. This conveys that your home life is essentially a free-for-all and that any kind of behavior is acceptable there. What's more, it leads each of you to repeat behaviors the others may find uncomfortable, unbearable or, quite possibly, appalling. It also means that you've left the gate to the fence which protects our stepfamily structure swinging in the breeze. Under those conditions, virtually anyone can saunter in and disrupt the harmony you're trying so hard to create.

Allowing emotionally-draining people (i.e., intrusive ex-spouses, unruly stepkids, prying in-laws, unsupportive "friends") to traipse in and out of your lives at will—whether in-person, online or otherwise—is a huge mistake. Yet, we've all done it! At some point or another, we've put off setting boundaries or failed to clearly define them. We may even put off setting House Rules out of fear that we'll ruffle a few feathers or end up looking like the bad guy. Without those mechanisms in place, however, we become doormats.

People then feel, believe and act as if they can: walk all over us, repeatedly disrespect us and fail to take us seriously. I know I've asked myself more than once (and not just as a stepmom): "Wait—what's the deal here?!" What's missing is typically a clear sense of *why* boundaries and House Rules are necessary, *when* to establish them and *how* they benefit not just us but everyone around us. Being "nice" should never overrule our need to love ourselves and to take our own needs seriously. You have to get to a point where you can confidently say, "Stop! Enough already. I won't take this anymore." Sound familiar? Well, there is a solution. There are several, in fact.

Unhealthy Boundaries & Boundary Violations

Addressing the *why*, *when* and *how* of boundary setting doesn't just benefit you. It benefits your entire stepfamily. It does that by ensuring that only those with a genuine need to know, or a direct stake in your stepfamily's short- and long-term successes, are granted access to its inner workings. As the one taking action, by reading this book, you hold the key to the gate that will keep everyone else out. Your partner, by extension of you, also holds a key to your stepfamily compound. Children and stepchildren of all ages have a role to play, as gatekeepers, though their responsibilities will vary and likely increase as they grow from toddlers into adolescents, teens and young adults.

The first thing I want you to do is to mentally close and lock that gate. (Go ahead, I'll wait.) For the time being, don't let anyone or anything get past you. This is a time for reflection and assessment, during which distractions will only serve to complicate matters further. Now, ask yourself how you feel when your own explicit or implied boundaries are violated. Does being the recipient of disrespect build you up? Or does it tear you down? Does being trod over leave you feeling mentally and physically vibrant? Or do you find it exhausting?

Without a clear sense of boundaries, our self-worth declines. We feel as if we're unworthy of respect. We feel drained, confused and upset. Resentment and anger then build up and rise within us. If our husbands or children make requests of us, when we're in a state like this one, we feel as if they're being unfairly demanding of our time and energy. We've let so many other people trample over our thoughts, hopes and dreams that there seems to be little joy left (or little to be found) in being a wife, a mother or a stepmother. We reach the end of our ropes quickly.

If this has happened or is happening to you, view it as a sign that you're either operating under: a lack of boundaries, a set of unhealthy boundaries or a set of boundaries which have gone unenforced for far too long and have been violated— over and over again. You, in turn, feel violated. That's a natural response. It's also healthy, in that you now recognize it and can use it as motivation to put the right kinds of boundaries in place. From here, you can begin to keep those things from ever happening again.

Signs that unhealthy boundaries are in place:

- Letting others define you
- Hinting, whining or implying
- Pleading, demanding or threatening
- Giving or taking (at will) without thinking
- Expecting others to fill our needs automatically

There are others, for sure. Have you ever compromised your personal rights or values, in order to please your partner? Do you say, "No," to the kids only to feel guilty about it later? Do you speak up when the ex treats you poorly? Do you know anyone who "falls apart" on cue or at the drop of a hat, expecting someone else to pick up the pieces and soothe them? Teens and others who accept advances from or "fall in love" quickly with people they barely know, whom they may not even like very much, do so in reaction to unhealthy boundaries of their own.

Examples of unhealthy stepfamily boundaries include:

- Oversharing with the (step-)children
- Behaving more like a friend than a parent
- Saying, "Yes," when what you mean is, "No"
- Seeking acceptance from your stepkids at all costs
- Sucking it up or stepping back to avoid confrontation

As stepmoms, we've all experienced these—and *far* worse—circumstances to some degree. We've cancelled plans with friends (or commitments of our own) to supervise our spouses' kids. We've listened as their Mom, in hopes of drumming up sympathy, "let it slip" that their Dad now pays less in child support or is taking her back to court for additional visitation rights. In your own bid to be the friendly martyr, you may have countered by badmouthing her to her kids while explaining why you and their Dad found it necessary to put new House Rules in place. While none of us relishes the resentment that sets in when we try to enforce boundaries the kids hate, none of these is helpful.

We're even prone to shelf our personal values so that we can gain greater acceptance from our stepkids. Remember that time your stepdaughter began going out with a much older guy and you failed to share your concerns over it? That's the kind of thing I'm talking about here. You may even fail to speak up when the stepkids disrespect you or when the ex badmouths you, not wanting to "cause a scene" or "make a big deal out of it." Yet, action is warranted and you're right to be concerned. Just remember that the other person's reaction is their responsibility; not yours.

Not everyone violates boundaries knowingly, by the way. That's why it's up to us to have firm boundaries in place from the get go. No one's a mind reader. Even psychics request validation, so they know they're at least getting warm. I challenge you, right now, to consider a time when you might have violated someone else's boundaries. Doing this will give you the perspective you need to recognize how important it is to communicate with others, so that the relationships you create within your stepfamily will be based on mutual trust, respect and consideration.

Ways we violate one another's boundaries:

- Withholding or distorting information
- Interrupting others when they're speaking
- Spending more than we originally agreed upon
- Invading someone's privacy or sharing their secrets
- Ignoring a spouse's request to call if we plan to work late

These aren't just adult concerns, though some do require adult intervention. We must certainly take action when a grownup behaves seductively in the company of a child or tries to engage them in conversations or activities which are inappropriate given their age or vulnerability level. Still, there are some instances in which our children and stepchildren are prone to push their siblings' and/or half-siblings' buttons—either knowingly or inadvertently.

Ways children violate each other's boundaries:

- Raiding one another's snack food stashes
- Eavesdropping on peer-to-peer talk/activity
- Tattling or failing to keep a secret in confidence
- "Borrowing" (toys, clothes, etc.) without asking first
- Snooping in one another's drawers, closets, diaries, etc.

As you start setting healthy boundaries in your home, consider all of these and the many other ways violating one another's boundaries deteriorates the quality of your stepfamily relationships. The goal, for you and your partner, is to set boundaries which take into account everyone's vulnerabilities and to then protect each of you against being taken advantage of or mistreated. And, trust me, I know that dealing with conflict between stepsiblings is no fun. In fact, it causes more personal and marital strain than it does in intact nuclear, or first, families.

Why is that? Well, because:

- Stepkids often move between homes.
- Different values and House Rules apply.
- There's a constant need for readjustment.
- Stepkids wish there was greater consistency.
- Parents may set loose boundaries out of guilt.

Still, addressing violations needn't cause a confrontation. In fact, having House Rules in place and holding fast to any consequences you and your partner have clearly defined and communicated increases trust within your home. Conversely, an absence of clear boundaries, House Rules and consequences you're willing to enforce increases mistrust, misunderstanding and distrust—which is an altogether absence of trust. The more you and your partner avoid setting and enforcing boundaries, in fact, the more your confidence levels will drop. You'll find it harder to trust yourselves, one another, your parenting skills and your individual roles. I can't stress that enough. So, it's better to have *balanced* boundaries in place than too few or too many.

Too Few or Too Many Boundaries

What do you think happens when you have too *few* boundaries in place? Or too *many*? You laid the groundwork for arriving at your own answers to these questions above, by making time to reflect on and assess the current state of your stepfamily relationships. You've mulled over the many ways boundaries have either hindered you or continue to hold you back from making real, lasting progress. It's now time to crack open the door to your stepfamily home and peek outside, unlocking that gate with increased confidence while continuing to guard it with a watchful eye.

Too few boundaries often find us dealing with aggressive kids who feel they're entitled to do whatever want, whenever they want. If pushing you to your breaking point is something that happens with regularity, your (step-)children have likely grown accustomed to seeing how far they can get before you, your partner and/or their other parent(s) tell them to stop—and keep them from repeating those behaviors, by way of reliable consequences.

Signs that too few boundaries exist:

- Stress within your adult/child relationship(s)
- Ambiguity about your relationship(s) and role(s)
- Misunderstandings in your adult/child relationship(s)
- Uneasiness or discomfort in your adult/child relationship(s)
- Uncommunicated or unrealistic expectations which incite conflict

Separation and divorce can lead parents to feel guilty and ashamed, resulting in a resistance to set and enforce boundaries even when it's clear they're necessary to healthy child development and (step-)parent/(step-)child interactions. Parents and stepparents then experience friction in their couples' relationships, with the parent wanting to be more lenient and the stepparent craving more structure. If we fail to strike a balance between what it is we both need and desire, in order to feel like effective role models, this can lead to hurt feelings and cause major rifts.

By themselves, separation and divorce lead children to feel confused and uncertain. At one point, they knew they were to rely on Mom and Dad for guidance. Now, with separate homes and maybe a stepmom and/or stepdad in the picture, they're not quite sure who to trust or who they should defer to. Stepmoms need the support of their partners, who must make certain that their children understand that we're now part of the equation and have a say in what goes on in our homes. If they fail to communicate support for us, their children have little reason to trust or obey us.

Another consequence of too few boundaries is not being able to distinguish where one person ends and the other begins. The stepchild who's been brought up to speed on all of the "terrible things" their father or stepmother has done to make their mother feel alone and isolated gets caught in a loyalty bind and is likely to become enmeshed, or entangled, in adult situations. The lines become very blurry for them. Do they side with Mom? Or do they form their own opinions of Dad and Stepmom? This dynamic isn't exclusive to ex-wives and their children, by the way.

Dads and their daughters, stepmoms and their sons—we all risk creating situations in which our kids find it difficult to individuate. It's possible you find it difficult to separate concerns of your own from those of your husband. We want to back one another up, but we shouldn't do it at our own detriment or for fear that we'll make a decision that's counter to other person's beliefs or preferences. Still, it's never okay to transfer our feelings onto our children or to burden them by treating them as confidants or adult substitutes. They are not our friends, partners or therapists.

At the other extreme, too many boundaries can be equally perplexing and harmful. At best, initiating and holding fast to too many rules makes daily life a grind. With little if any room for negotiation, others find that there are no right answers and few options available to them. Feeling as if they're trapped, they can't help but react uncomfortably. This drives home the point that the surest way to make others feel powerless is to run a household under absolute rule. Partners and stepchildren are then driven to defy us to see if we'll uphold all of those rules.

Signs that too many boundaries exist:

- A tense, rigid home environment
- A lack of openness and negotiation
- A sensation of "walking on eggshells"
- A ban on making independent decisions
- A fear (or inability) to share opinions freely

When there are too many boundaries in place, it's a sign that one person is trying to control the others. There is a need to dominate so that others simply do what you say with little to no regard for their own wants or needs. Rigid boundaries keep others from experiencing a sense of individuality, rob them of personal space in which to discover who they are and leave them feeling insecure. With no ability to make choices of their own, their thoughts and feelings align with everyone else's— out of fear that they'll be chided, criticized or worse for being themselves.

Healthy Stepfamily Boundaries & House Rules

"Life is really simple, but we insist on making it complicated." – Confucius

Maybe the topic of boundary setting is new to you. Or, perhaps, you're looking to revamp your stepfamily's House Rules. For all I know, it could be that you have boundaries and House Rules in place and are just unsure whether what you're using now is working at all or giving you the best possible results. Whatever your situation, it's always good to periodically review your stepfamily's value system and beliefs. My guess is you'll find that what you started out with doesn't make sense anymore or fails to hold true now that your stepfamily has grown and evolved.

A great first step, in setting healthy stepfamily boundaries and House Rules, is to open up a dialogue. Survey your own thoughts and question the other people in your home, establishing a framework of common values everyone is willing and able to abide by. By taking time to identify your shared values, you and your spouse will be better equipped to create boundaries which help everyone feel heard, understood and valued. You'll also create a dynamic in which everyone knows and understands how they affect everyone else's health, happiness and safety.

When discussing your stepfamily's boundaries and House Rules:

- Ask everyone to cite their primary, unmet needs.
- Ask, too, what may be causing problem(s).
- Make a list of each person's concerns.
- Prioritize those needs, as a family.
- Make a pact to address them.

There's no way to solve all of your stepfamily's problems overnight. By beginning with a list of primary needs, you open the door to future Stepfamily Meetings. Use those as a way to check in, see how things are going and decide what other steps might need to be taken. Rather than include everyone in the boundary-setting process, use your notes from this initial meeting to guide a brainstorming session with your partner. Still, do set a date and time for a follow-up Stepfamily Meeting— during which you'll share a list of related boundaries and consequences.

If a particular topic is of immediate concern, set and communicate a related House Rule and consequences on the spot or later that day/evening. Agree to address all other concerns within a set time frame: two days, two weeks, etc. Just be sure to give you and your partner enough time to really dig into what your individual concerns are and what the most appropriate consequences would be for failing to uphold any new House Rules. As you address each one, aim to balance your adult opinions with solutions you know your stepchildren are capable of helping you uphold.

If getting started is difficult, begin by identifying:

- (1) personal boundary you have now + (1) you wish you had
- (1) household boundary you have now + (1) you wish you had
- (1) adult/child boundary you have now + (1) you wish you had

In our own stepfamily home, personal space was often a point of contention for me. I knew I wanted and needed time to myself, as well as a place to put my things where I knew they would be safe from prying eyes and hands. This truly was a priority for me. I communicated that without pointing fingers or singling out anyone who may have violated my personal space previously. Working together, Bernard and I then: set what we felt were fair boundaries around it, attached a consequence to future violations and communicated all of that to our kids.

Involving our children and making sure they understood the problem led to greater acceptance when we then put a solution in place. Everyone acknowledged it, during our own follow-up Stepfamily Meeting, ensuring that we all understood the new protocol and associated expectations. This led to increased order, peace, harmony and security in our stepfamily home. Did the kids test our boundaries? Sure! Yet, establishing them with the kids' help allowed Bernard and me to stand firm while avoiding any "us against them" discord.

For the best results, give everyone in your stepfamily time to adapt to new ways of being and collaborating. That includes letting the children *feel* and *express* any emotions that come with being disappointed, angry, sad or upset by changes in policy. As parents and stepparents, we instinctively want our kids to feel better. But that can keep us from setting healthy boundaries and teaching them what's okay and what's not okay—so that they grow into caring, responsible and considerate adults. Keep this in mind when dealing with adult (step-)children, too, as a need for boundaries is ongoing: "We want you to visit us. We just ask that you call before popping over."

Expect some pushback from your stepkids, your own kids and others (i.e., exes, in-laws, family friends). While they may not express enthusiasm, it's not your job to make everyone around you happy. And, believe me, I'm not talking about being selfish, self-absorbed or narcissistic here. Healthy boundaries have nothing to do with narcissism. Quite the opposite is true. Setting boundaries shows love and concern for your kids, your stepkids, your partner, yourself and anyone who interacts with your stepfamily. Good working boundaries serve as proof that you care enough to do what's important and necessary to keep everyone reasonably happy, healthy and safe from harm.

As I've said before, you are *in no way* responsible for other people's emotions. This doesn't mean it's alright to be hurtful or mean. Not at all. You can and are wise to remain empathetic to the kids' concerns. It's natural they'd want to do certain things which may be inappropriate for their ages or out of sync with your stepfamily's values. It's part of growing up. Don't ridicule, bully or otherwise demean them for it. Don't soothe them, either, by giving in. Same goes for any exes in your life. It's not your or your partner's responsibility to soothe their hurt or upset feelings.

When you say, "No," stand by it. Do this knowing they'll likely react to your newfound ability to erect a fence that protects and guards you against harm or abuse. When you know that what you're doing is in the best interest of yourself and your family, you won't feel the least bit guilty and you won't need to seek justification or agreement from others in order to feel good about your decision. Always do what's right rather than what's popular. It may be that someone else's feelings do get hurt or that they feel insulted when you say, "No." That's them reacting to your willingness to set boundaries; ones which, remember, are there to nurture and protect you and your stepfamily. If you absolutely feel a need to respond when someone gets ruffled over you saying, "No," or when you stand up for yourself and your loved ones, be sure any reply you offer honors the boundaries you've created.

A few different responses you might offer include:

- This is what I'm okay with.
- This is what I'm *not* okay with.
- This is what I plan to do about it.
- This is what I think is best right now.
- This is my solution to what's happening.

Note, too, that you can and will want to set boundaries without closing yourself off to others. This is critical if you're to sustain caring, supportive relationships. At the same time, be careful to protect yourself against becoming a sponge or a magnet that sucks up everyone else's bad energy, foul moods or funky vibes. In other words, don't tolerate temper tantrums. Simply be firm and loving as you go about setting boundaries and discussing them with your spouse and/or stepchildren. If you feel your boundaries are about to be crossed, as you do that, ask your partner for help. Let him know you're there to back him up, too.

Let's imagine, though, that your husband is talking about how his ex is driving him up a wall. He can't stand her and wishes he'd never met her, he says. As his partner, you want to be supportive and you want to listen to his concerns. You might even want to take on some of his pain, alleviating his frustration. This is a bad idea. By taking on your husband's anger and frustration over his ex, you prevent him from being accountable for his own emotions and from directly addressing the issue with her. In effect, you're trying to save him from himself.

Here's the deal: He needs to feel those emotions and he needs to own up to them. When you're angry with and frustrated at your stepkids, it's your responsibility to own up to those emotions. When they're angry or frustrated with you, he should teach them, it's their responsibility to respectfully bring those issues to your attention. Our behaviors are something else altogether. How we react in response to uncomfortable feelings is our own responsibility to manage. We learn to do this well by tackling a variety of difficult situations head-on.

Setting healthy boundaries around negativity is important. If it feels right to you, agree to listen to your husband's rants but decide for how long and how frequently. If he continues to rehash the same issue over and over again, then it's time to let him know that you've listened long enough. You're willing to support him but now he needs to take action. Moaning and groaning about how angry or frustrated we feel changes nothing. I view this as sitting in a rocking chair, rocking back and forth over and over again, thinking something is going to change. Nothing will.

Intense anger and frustration, on the other hand, are signals that something is seriously wrong. It may even be time to seek professional help. After all, it's hard to see the solutions which are right in front of us when we're mired in an issue. What does that have to do with the topic of boundaries? Or, for that matter, respect? While they're still learning to navigate the world, it can be common for children to push our buttons. As an adult, your job is to teach them to demonstrate respect while appreciating your right and other people's right to say, "No," to their requests.

Say your stepson wants to go over to his friend's house after school and promises to do his chores when he gets back. If he's made this promise before and didn't follow through, you'd be right to say, "No. I need you to do your chores now. Then you can go to your friend's house." You still can't control whether or not he does those chores, but you can control what you'll do if he doesn't. Maybe he'll lose his cell phone privileges, be grounded during his next visit with you or have to do without clean clothes—since, like him, you don't feel like doing your own chores.

I can hear you now: "Wait a minute, Claudette! The backlash we'll get from the ex on that one is too much." To that I say, "He's in *your* home." You don't need to justify your choice to anyone but his father. Though, ideally, you and your partner would have already mapped out your boundaries and consequences on this issue. You also don't need for the ex to be in agreement with you in order to feel good about whether a decision you've made is in your stepfamily's best interest. This is the embodiment of doing what's right rather than what's popular.

I have an example that involves end-of-the-year holidays, which many stepfamilies find tough to juggle. Bernard's mother had complained that we didn't spend enough time with her, so we began traveling 600 miles (one way) to make her happy. Still, it wasn't enough. Despite the fact that we rushed around to fit everything in, making sure his girls also got time with their mom and my son also got time with his dad, no one was happy. The more we tried, the more miserable we became. Finally, Bernard and I drew up a holiday contract that made it easier on us and the kids.

When it comes to setting healthy stepfamily boundaries and House Rules, I have one final bit of advice. Accept that you'll have to express your wants and needs many times over, during the course of your relationships, as no one gets it right the first time. Think back to when you first hopped on a bike. Were you able to ride it that very first time? Most likely, you weren't. You probably fell several times, scraping your knees and hands in the process. You got up and tried again, right? It's the same with setting boundaries. It takes practice to define them. It takes even more practice to enforce them. Don't give up because your spouse or stepkids resist your initial attempts. Try, try again.

One day you may find yourself coasting down the road with eyes closed and arms open wide!

CHAPTER 11

Stepfamily Challenges, House Rules & Consequences

A side from the individual, the family is the most basic unit of society. Within each of our families, we hope to and can certainly expect to feel secure, understood and supported. After all, families themselves are teams of individuals who not only share House Rules; depending on the unique roles they play, everyone within that family also shares varying degrees of responsibility for one another. And, when yours functions well, other aspects of your life tend to run more smoothly. Individual goals may even become family goals with everyone working to ensure they're met.

In stepfamilies, however, teamwork and collaboration aren't always apparent. Nor are they built right in. This is especially the case in the early stages of stepfamily formation. Despite having boundaries in place, problem areas are bound to arise or may persist long after we've grown weary of them. Yet, no matter what your stepfamily's specific structure looks like, the ideal approach is to be respectful of one another and work together on common goals. That's why it's important to set House Rules and establish roles everyone can refer to.

In stepfamilies, it's additionally important that those things foster a sense of belonging. This is true whether you and your other stepfamily members live together full-time, part-time or only occasionally. Putting a good foundation in place gives everyone a template to work from and reinforces a sense of belonging, by showing care and concern for each of your needs when you're together. In my experience—as a stepfamily coach, a stepmother and a mother myself—second and subsequent family households run more smoothly when expectations are established right from the start. Open and honest communication is the binding agent that then holds your foundation, your couple's relationship and your stepfamily together. That includes using open, honest dialogue to get through the tough spots.

You and your partner must make time to consider situations which are unique to your stepfamily dynamic, as well as those which nearly every stepfamily deals with at one point or another. By facing these challenges head-on and with age-appropriate help from any children who are involved, you'll be better positioned to address potential problem areas and to ensure that your stepfamily's House Rules, individual member roles and related responsibilities reflect reality. This will keep you all moving ahead and will help you avoid getting stuck in negative or self-defeating thought/behavior patterns on your way to brighter days.

Types of challenges which are specific to stepfamilies:

- Dealing with the ex, whether "friend or foe"
- Funding his/her kids' educations, including college
- Navigating custody, visitation and pick-ups/drop-offs
- Setting guidelines for financial support and inheritances
- Kids' reactions to remarriage, "ours" babies, adoptions, etc.
- Deciding how kids will refer to stepparents and extended family

That first point raises all sorts of questions by itself. If the breakup was amicable or the children's biological parents can at least be cordial toward one another, co-parenting may work. If hostilities exist, perhaps parallel or disengaged parenting is a better choice. Then, too, there's a need to mesh—or, at a minimum, agree to disagree over—your and your partner's unique parenting styles and the roles you'll each play when it comes to supervising one another's children. Stepfamily experts typically agree that primary disciplinary responsibility falls on the biological parent's shoulders.

When it comes to parenting styles and roles, however, you and your partner will first need to discuss what your individual roles will be within your stepfamily. This is something you should do in private, though you'll eventually share this information with any children who are part of your stepfamily household. For example, when Dad's away, the kids need to know that Stepmom is empowered to enforce the House Rules. If you happen to be both his kids' Stepmom and Mom to your own children, the opposite is true. Your kids need to know that Stepdad will be doing likewise.

Doling out consequences, though, is likely to be more contentious for the non-biological parent.

Other things to discuss, as a couple:

- Your individual expectations of each other
- Your individual expectations of the children
- Your needs, regarding effective (step-)parenting
- Your (step-)parenting styles and how they may differ
- Your roles, as they affect (step-)parent/(step-)child relations

Parenting styles are widely regarded as falling into one of four categories: *Authoritarian, Authoritative, Permissive* or *Uninvolved.* Stepparent roles are equally varied and range from serving as a confidant, friend, mentor, parental figure or role model to your stepchildren. In your household, you might even serve as some combination of those. To avoid confusing the children, it's best to get clear about how you both will be involved in their lives and to then adhere (as closely as possible) to your defined roles. This makes it easier to support one another, too.

I suggest that you first research and write down what your own parenting style is. Have your partner do the same. Then, figure out how you can leverage your differences to provide everyone in your home with the best possible forms of guidance and support. Take similar steps after reviewing the list of common stepparent roles above. It may help to list the qualities you already possess, as stepparents, and to add to that any skills you'd like to develop more fully. Finally, if you could have it your way, what kind of parent and/or stepparent would you *truly* like to be?

Let all of that guide both your behavior and your answers to the questions appearing in the Appendix [see "Arriving at Must-Have House Rules: What does stepfamily life look like to you—the (step-)parents?"], which are designed to get you and your partner operating on the same wavelength. Don't spend too much time analyzing any one question. In writing, simply answer each one in a way that you believe makes sense for your stepfamily.

Once you and your partner have answered each question, thank one another for participating openly and honestly. Then, one-by-one, discuss your answers. There are no "right" or "wrong" answers. If you disagree on a topic, you simply have different ways of looking at things. Based on what you each want and need for your stepfamily, try to arrive at a compromise. If you can't do that, come back to it later.

This is also a great strategy for resolving conflict: Speak your truth and try to compromise. If you can't, take a break. Revisit the topic at an agreed-upon date and time.

If the children are old enough to have a stake and a say in these things, include them in the conversation. However, I strongly urge you and your husband to first set aside some quiet time in which you can go through your list of questions and select those which are most appropriate to your stepfamily situation. To help with this, I've also included bonus questions well-suited to older kids, such as teens and young adults, in the Appendix. (See "Arriving at Must-Have House Rules: Kids, what does stepfamily life look like to you?")

Setting, Implementing & Enforcing House Rules

Whose job is it to set House Rules, implement them and enforce them in your stepfamily home? For House Rules to be truly effective, it's up to both of you—the biological parent and the stepparent—to create the initial set of House Rules and to outline any responsibilities which are tied to them. Do this in private, when you have ample time to yourselves, so that any disagreements or squabbles over expectations and responsibilities won't be overheard.

The best time to establish House Rules is upfront, preferably before moving in together. If you're past that point, do it as early as possible in your stepfamily relationship. If that's today? So be it! The biological parent should lead any presentation of the House Rules to the rest of your family, especially when older children are involved. As the secondary disciplinarian, the stepparent should be included and should be identified as someone who's authorized to help enforce those rules. What follows are a few guidelines for having this discussion.

It's best to schedule weekly or bi-weekly stepfamily meetings at the onset, during which you'll discuss the House Rules in cooperation with any children they affect. The more involved they are in creating, implementing and upholding your rules, the more likely it is they'll also take ownership in the process. You can start by reviewing key rules. Then, mention what's working well. Finally, ask for feedback on what's not working well. Avoid pointing fingers, though, since you don't want to alienate or embarrass anyone in particular.

House Rules Stepfamily Meeting guidelines:

- Make it clear that the adults run the meeting.
- Ask your (step-)children to help set consequences.
- Be sure everyone demonstrates respect for one another.
- Solicit the kids' input, but make all final decisions yourselves.
- Use any existing or prior House Rules as a familiar starting point.

(10) Stepfamily House Rules worth implementing:

- Honesty is a must for everyone.
- At night, it's lights out by ___ p.m.
- Homework is to be done by ___ p.m.
- Beds will be made prior to eating breakfast.
- "Please," and, "Thank you," are non-negotiable.
- Clean laundry is to be put away within ___ day(s).
- Curfew is ___ p.m. for [Name] and ___ p.m. for [Name].
- Jackets and backpacks will be hung up [specify where].
- Outdoor shoes are to be taken off and left [specify where].
- Dad will discipline but Stepmom shares authority with him.

Special topics you can turn to for other ideas:

- Privacy in your own home
- Privacy between the kids' homes
- Personal, physical and emotional boundaries
- Household chores, fairness and individual responsibility
- Respectful (step-)sibling and (step-)child/(step-)parent interaction

Once your stepfamily's House Rules and related consequences have been defined, you can begin to enforce them. Be sure you've clearly communicated both of these to your stepfamily members. If you expect serious kickback, have everyone sign an "agreement" at the close of your Stepfamily Meeting. In addition, post major House Rules where everyone can see them. (The fridge is always popular!) Chore lists can be posted on the corresponding children's bedroom doors. If certain chores involve cleaning common areas or kids'-only spaces, such as shared bathrooms, consider posting them there instead.

When it comes to enforcement, strive to always be: consistent, specific and timely. If a given consequence—whether it's meant to follow positive or negative behavior—

seems to be out of step with reality, have a discussion with your partner and arrive at a better fit. Then, have him communicate the change to his children and do the same for any children of your own. This drives home the notion that your House Rules will remain flexible enough to ensure that they fit your current situation and are designed to account for changes in your stepfamily dynamic, particularly as children grow up to be teens or young adults.

This entire process is designed to teach your family members to function well within the home and in the world at large. House Rules give your stepfamily much-needed structure and encourage everyone to be more productive, cooperative and considerate. If you or your spouse slip up, learn from your mistakes. Be willing, as needed, to apologize for any behavior you've displayed which is out of sync with your House Rules or shared values. In other words, take an adult approach to being responsible and accountable by modeling behaviors you expect from others.

Consequences

For some, the mere thought of a "consequence" implies that something bad is headed their way. They then avoid any situation or circumstance which would land them in hot water. This is what makes consequences so effective. For others, the thought of having to confront or deal with the outcome of a consequence is too much to bear. As a result, they avoid doing them altogether. People who fail to parent well out of guilt fall into that last category. Yet, in order for boundaries and House Rules to be effective, we must put consequences in place. Otherwise? They're useless.

Think back to that fence we've been talking about. If you put up a fence of protection around your stepfamily but leave the gate wide open, so that nearly anyone can come and go as they please, what's the point of having a fence in the first place? Sure, they might initially be wary about trespassing. But, once they realize nothing will happen as a result, they just come on through. After all, if no one's minding the gate, there's no reason to respect your right to privacy. There's also little incentive to take note of other cues intended to keep them at bay.

Boundaries need to be clearly and explicitly defined in order for other people to know what to expect when they trample over them. This is especially true when you're in the process of merging two families. You and your partner are coming at this from different perspectives and different cultures, so to speak, but you both hold the expectation of creating a new family unit (or community) in which everyone adapts to a new or revised set of rules. Know, too, that what you think is "common sense" may not be someone else's idea of common sense. In fact, assuming everyone thinks the way you do can set you up for a major disaster.

Too, consequences impact everyone in your stepfamily system—not just those they're directly aimed at—and are not meant to serve as punishment but as natural reactions to, or outcomes associated with, certain actions and behaviors. If you have to label them, I guess you could say they can be "good" or "bad." For example, if you perform well in your work and deliver great results, you can expect something good to happen: You get a bonus, some form of praise or a raise in salary. That would be a natural, positive consequence to having a strong work ethic. This type of reward system can be replicated in your home, as well.

If the kids do their chores with regularity, maybe they'll earn extra privileges or additional spending money. If they gossip, breaking boundaries by sharing personal stories they have no place sharing with others, maybe they'll have privileges or future allowance money taken away from them. Still, what one person finds offensive another person may not: talking loudly, making bodily noises on purpose, singing at the dinner table, etc. House Rules are intended to define what's okay and what's not okay. They also help you identify which behaviors will be rewarded and which will be discouraged, by way of consequences and enforcement.

After defining your stepfamily's boundaries and House Rules, ask:

- Who did we set these for?
- What's their ongoing purpose?
- Who'll play a role in enforcing them?
- How will we know if they're not enforced?
- Will they keep our stepfamily safe from harm?

When children fail to learn or experience healthy parental boundaries, they become uncertain and hesitant. Their interactions with others are marked by insecurity and they have a difficult time developing trust in themselves and in those around them. When parents establish known and firm boundaries, especially for young children, the outcomes are more positive. Those children feel more secure and grow up learning to more easily identify and respect the boundaries of others within the home and outside of your home.

If your stepfamily's boundaries remain unclear and go unenforced, you can expect: your requests of the children to be met with confusion, your expectations to go unfulfilled and your general mood to border on being closer to frustration than satisfaction. You're basically setting yourselves up to experience more conflict than is necessary, given that your values and beliefs will go unspoken and your desire for harmony or orderliness will be unexpressed. Yet, if your boundaries are articulated and backed up by consequences, you'll all gain greater trust in one another.

It's important to note that any consequences you set today should remain flexible. That's because, if the boundaries you and your spouse set for the kids wind up being too rigid or impossible to work with, you'll want to make some changes. If you don't, it's likely that at least one member of your family will wind up feeling isolated, frustrated and/or alone in their struggle to measure up.

As you carry out a consequence for a boundary that is working, remain calm but resolute. Let's say one of the children acts out or pleads to say up "just five minutes" longer. Rather than react harshly, stop what you're doing and plainly say, "Sorry. Bedtime is bedtime." Then escort them up to their room, making small talk that has nothing to do with staying up late. The boundary is still in place and you're sticking to it. You're behaving reasonably, as the adult in this scenario, rather than flying off the handle. You're making it safe for the child to test the boundary without giving in to them. You mean what you say and are walking the walk. This does much more to create a sense of security for your stepkids than giving in ever could.

Congratulations! You just proved that you can be relied on to stay true to your word. You've reinforced the child's understanding of what's expected of every member of your stepfamily, including those whose job it is to enforce its boundaries and House Rules. You've also set an example for your spouse and any other children in your home, by modeling enforcement in a way that's caring and empathetic—but to be expected. If the child struggles or talks back, you and your partner must make sure that any consequence for that is carried out. (If it's his kid, let him do the enforcing. If it's your kid, do the enforcing yourself.) This is how you earn others' respect and compliance.

To minimize potential objections, implement House Rules which:

- Encourage clarity and understanding.
- Minimize stress within your stepfamily.
- Make clear that everyone has a role to play.
- Take into account prior House Rules/policies.
- Promote realistic expectations and consequences.

Think of your boundaries and House Rules as basic guidelines for respectful behavior. Think of consequences and enforcement as ways in which they're demonstrated, unifying your stepfamily through a sense of community which has rules in place to ensure that everyone's needs are met. We all crave a sense of belonging in our lives and in our homes. Stepfamilies simply need to work harder at this, since their histories are intertwined with standards which were set long ago (when the prior family was intact) and since children often lament the loss of the familiar.

Show—Don't Tell

Do as I say, not as I do! Right? While growing up, my parents' twist on it was: "Don't do as I do. Do as I say!" My mom would tell us not to smoke cigarettes, saying it was bad for us. All the while, she held a lit cigarette between her fingers. (I'm dating myself a bit here, I know.) I'm sure you've experienced inconsistencies of this nature in your own life. It's confusing and leads to mistrust, since actions do speak louder than words. We can use this knowledge in our stepfamily homes to ensure better understanding and commitment when it comes to boundaries.

Ways you can show vs. tell them what to do:

- Keep your House Rules simple.
- Keep all requests upbeat and moderate.
- Be as specific as you can, so there's no guessing.
- Make all consequences relevant, teachable moments.
- Be open but resist negotiating with anyone but your partner.

We've talked lots about boundaries and House Rules as they relate primarily to the stepchildren in your home. We even discussed ways to enforce them and explored a few examples which could be common to your own experience. Yet, what about your partner? Are there boundaries and rules you'd like him to follow when it comes to interacting with you? Just as the kids won't know what you expect of them unless you express yourself and follow through with consequences, your spouse won't know what you expect of him unless you open up and voice those concerns.

Many stepmoms tell me that their husbands spend an inordinate amount of time talking with their exes about issues which could "easily" be taken care of by email or in brief conversations. So, that's the example I'll use here. Say John gets a call from his ex-wife, Heather, nearly every day that's almost always about something his kids did at home or at school. Heather insists she needs John to "deal with it *right now*." She can't seem to do anything about it and the kids won't listen to her. While he and Jennifer had dinner plans, he asks to cancel so he can go to Heather's house and talk with his kids about whatever's gone wrong. Disappointed, Jennifer begrudgingly says, "Yeah, sure."

This is a good example of there not being healthy boundaries in *either* home. Although John wants to do what's right by his kids, he's also not making Heather accountable for dealing with issues which arise in *her* home during *her* time with the kids. Instead, he's letting her delegate those problems to him. Beyond blurring the lines between what he's responsible for and what Heather's responsible for (in everyone's eyes, including the kids'), John's not demonstrating respect for Date Night with his current wife, Jennifer. As it is, Jennifer feels she gets very little time with her husband. His "need" to put out fires in the other home is just one reason for this—but it's a recurring one.

Should John *not* get involved? Yes and no. His children are his first responsibility. But that's also the case for his ex, Heather. John could, however, raise the issue with his kids the next time he sees them. Heather is further minimizing her authority over (and any respect she might command from) her children by having Dad come to the rescue, so he can then resolve or take care of issues which originate in her home. When John finally makes it home to Jennifer, he feels he has little time or energy left to be an engaging husband to her or an active stepparent to her children.

After hours spent at the other home, all John wants to do is relax and not hear any more about it. Yet, by now, Jennifer's livid that he spent hours on end interacting with Heather and wants her "fair share" of his attention. What's the solution? John needs to set healthier boundaries with Heather. And pronto! He needs to tell her exactly which issues, if any, he's willing to be involved in or hear about and how frequently. In addition, he needs to be clear about when he's willing to respond to those issues: "When the kids are with me next," or, "By Monday."

Will Heather resist? Likely. She's used to being rescued by John, though that doesn't make it okay. Jennifer plays a role here, too. Without being snarky, she can insist that John set reasonable guidelines he then expects Heather to abide by. Yes, life is full of exceptions, but exceptions are rare. They don't happen monthly, weekly or daily. Jennifer must also stop saying, "Yeah, sure," and instead tell John that these disruptions are hurtful. She can calmly explain that they compromise her ability to trust him to take her, their relationship and their time together seriously.

John needs to know that only *after* he sets a boundary with Heather will he and Jennifer be able to focus their efforts on strengthening their marriage and couple's bond. If he doesn't, he's contributing to their demise. His decision to be firm with Heather going forward will have the added benefit of allowing his kids to experience a safe, secure and less complicated home life on both fronts. It will also ease Jennifer's feelings of jealousy and resentment, which were mounting bit-by-bit until she almost couldn't stand the mention of Heather's name or her stepkids' names.

Clearly, demonstrating and upholding healthy boundaries requires concerted effort on everyone's part. That's true whether it comes to how our *own* children are to be treated, how our stepchildren are to be treated, how our relationships are to be treated or how we're to be treated. As equal partners in our relationships, we stepmoms are responsible for being open and honest with our partners. We must share our feelings with them and set boundaries of our own around any behaviors we're willing to tolerate and unwilling to tolerate.

For all we know, Jennifer has never shared her anger over this maddening circumstance with John. Instead, she expects him to magically "know" how she wants to be treated. While we've all been there, let me set the record straight once and for all: In cases like this one, telling *versus* showing may be the exception to the rule. So, don't be like Jennifer. Don't say, "Yeah, sure," when what you really mean is: "Uh, please, no." Or, more succinctly, "No."

Your relationship is at stake. Without that, why bother reading this book at all?!

CHAPTER 12

Setting Rules & Boundaries— Together!

T he stepfamily professionals I'm regularly in contact with all agree that the best time to establish House Rules and boundaries is as early on as possible in your couple's relationship. More specifically, you and your partner would have addressed these topics *before* moving in together.

First, you would have set potential House Rules and boundaries as a couple, in private. Then, you would have discussed what it is you both want or need to see happen to encourage a home life that promotes safety, security and respect for everyone involved. Finally, you would have arrived at a good working draft of House Rules and boundaries which could be shared with, understood by and adhered to by each of the children in your care. If you somehow bypassed all of that, rest easy. It's never too late to come together and make it happen.

In preparation, ask yourselves two key questions:

1. Do House Rules and boundaries exist already?
2. Either way, whose job is it to set and implement House Rules and boundaries on behalf of our stepfamily?

In the best case scenario, the biological parent is the one to finalize, communicate and implement House Rules and boundaries in your stepfamily home. This is especially important when there are older or savvier children involved. Stepparents like you then take on the role of showing support for and enforcing those things.

This strategy is supported by decades of research, including that conducted by Psychologist, Family Therapist and Couples Therapist Patricia L. Papernow, EdD—the director of the Institute for Stepfamily Education since 2010 and the author of numerous studies and publications, such as *Recoupling in Mid-life and Beyond* and *Blended Families*.

"Find both boundaries and compassion," Papernow told me recently. "One without the other doesn't work so well."

"The research is *very* clear," she emphasized. "Until or unless stepchildren feel they have a trusting and caring relationship with a stepparent, parents must be the limit-setters. Stepparents do need to have input but parents need to have *final* say about their own kids. And parents need to be the ones to set the limits; not stepparents."

Yet, why is that? And what can be done, in your own stepfamily, to ensure a smooth transition?

"The amount of time it takes for stepparents to build trusting, caring relationships varies by child," Papernow explained. "Boys and, in general, children eight years or younger often come around sooner. Girls, especially early teen girls, often need much more time (to adjust to the new dynamic). Also, kids caught in tough loyalty binds with their other parents may be unable to open up to their stepparents without feeling as if they are betraying their other parents."

"There are some very healthy and mature stepfamilies, by the way, in which stepparents *never* take a disciplinary role. This is especially true if they came along when their stepkids were already teenaged or older. Again, stepparents can have input and a say in these families. But parents continue to be the ones who do the limit setting."

While you needn't remain silent, she assured me, it helps to frame your own requests regarding House Rules, roles and boundaries in terms which are closer to, "I'd love it if x." That compared to, "You/they had better do such and such—or else." Too, as the Know > Like > Trust factor in your home increases, you may be able to expand your role as a disciplinarian stepparent and, if your partner is a stepparent to your own children, vice versa. If you do that, move forward cautiously or you risk undoing all of the work you've done to earn the kids' trust and respect thus far.

Dads, Stepmoms & Discipline

It can often be the case that moms do a lot of the disciplining in nuclear, or first, families. In my work as a stepmom coach, I've found that this tends to result in stepmoms being viewed with contempt or as otherwise "evil." This typically occurs if and when they try to fill mom-sized shoes within their respective stepfamilies. Since the kids don't know you as intimately as they do their mother, they're likely to rebuke your efforts to get them to do things they aren't accustomed to doing or simply don't want to do. Not without dad stepping in, anyhow.

This is why it's so important for their biological parent to take an active role in establishing and communicating your stepfamily House Rules and boundaries. If not, your efforts to enforce them will fall flat and you'll end up looking like the bad guy no matter how reasonable your requests are. Don't take this to mean that you should let yourself be disrespected or your opinions disregarded. What it does mean is that, in order to make everyone's lives easier (including your own), you should avoid disciplining your stepchildren as a way of letting Dad off the hook.

As their parent, he must take charge. As a parent yourself, if applicable, you must take charge and not expect your partner to establish limits for or discipline your own children. As you merge your families, you each need to be more involved than ever in taking ownership of your individual roles as disciplinarians. I encourage clients who *both* bring biological children into the mix to think of their stepfamilies as business mergers. It takes time to iron out the details, reach agreements and decide what to keep/discard—as you renegotiate roles, get the employees to agree, etc.

When the biological parent is absent, a stepparent is wise to view themselves as a caregiver or visiting relative who's been asked to enforce what's already in place. This truly is a matter of enforcement, ensuring that everyone abides by established and agreed-upon norms. If the children act up or talk back, do what's necessary to ensure everyone's safety. Afterward, discuss what went on with the biological parent. Do this in private, allowing him to take corrective steps and reinforce his support for any actions you took or decisions you made. If he doesn't agree with how you handled the situation, talk it out among yourselves and set future guidelines you can both agree to. What follows is one example you or someone you know may relate to pretty easily.

Stepmom: "The rule is homework *before* TV."
Stepchild: "You're not my parent."

Stepmom: "You're right. You have a Mom and you have a Dad. I'm not here to replace either of them. I know we're still getting to know each other, but right now I'm the adult in charge. And the House Rule is? No TV until homework is done. Feel free to ask your father about it when he gets home."

Sound familiar? I wouldn't be surprised if it did.

Communicating House Rules & Boundaries

It's not enough to set or establish House Rules and boundaries within your stepfamily home. They must also be communicated, understood and agreed to. One way to do that is through weekly, biweekly or monthly stepfamily meetings. Set time aside in which you can all discuss existing House Rules or introduce the children to either new sets of rules and boundaries or revised editions. It's not enough to say that something is a rule, "Because." Explain how your rules and boundaries impact the safety, security and/or privacy needs of everyone in your home.

Tailor your conversation so that it accounts for differences in the children's ages and/or developmental stages. Older children will have an easier time understanding House Rules and boundaries, though they may be more resistant to them. Still, involve everyone in the conversation to ensure buy-in across your entire stepfamily. If an issue needs to be addressed, by putting a House Rule in place, whenever possible involve the children in that process. While you and your partner should already know what you'd like to see happen, remain open-minded. The more involved your stepchildren are in creating and implementing rules, the more likely it is they'll participate in carrying them out.

Ownership is key. By giving them a stake in the outcome, your (step-)children are more likely to participate actively in the conversation. Still, it's up to the adults to run the meeting. If any changes need to be made or are requested with regard to new or existing rules and boundaries, discuss them as a couple—after your meeting has ended—and promise to get back to the children with the final word after you've had time to talk things over. I suggest giving yourselves at least 72 hours to do that before implementing changes which aren't critical or immediate.

Basic Stepfamily House Rules & Boundaries Meeting guidelines:

- Get everyone together at the appointed time.
- Review any existing rules and responsibilities.
- Present any new rules or changes you're considering.

- Hear the kids out and ask them to suggest consequences.
- Thank them, promise to make a decision soon and follow through.

This is simply a guide, as I've outlined additional steps below: *Step 1*, *Step 2*, etc. Think of setting House Rules and boundaries for your stepfamily as a way for you and your partner to ensure that what goes on in your home reflects everyone's shared values and beliefs. As parents and moderators, invite the children's input but clarify that any final decisions are yours to make—as a couple—on everyone's behalf. This is a good time, too, to remind them that you're in agreement over how they'll be enforced and that you *both* have the authority to enforce them.

Will this process be easy? I doubt it. What some call "blending" families is like merging two corporations: Planning, cooperation and communication are essential. From time to time, changes need to be made and rules need to be amended. So, anticipate an adjustment period. Expect a few, unintentional slip-ups. Show respect and concern for the children's ideas, taking them into serious consideration whenever you can. Be sure that everyone's opinions are heard and respected. Take turns listening and talking, maybe starting with the youngest and ending with the oldest.

For even greater acceptance, ask the children which chores they'd *like* to be responsible for. If they want to swap housekeeping roles and are capable of carrying them out, let them do it. When it comes to topics involving cooperation, explain what the consequences are for not doing one's part or respecting each other's boundaries. Set a predictable time and place for future meetings, so everyone knows they'll get to air their grievances and can rely on you to listen. Frame those meetings as a way to ensure that you all enjoy a healthy, ongoing routine.

Speaking of efficiency, ask that any new topics or concerns be brought to the parent's attention before the meeting. Heck, keep a suggestion box in your kitchen! Do whatever makes it easier for everyone to feel as if they have a say. You and your partner can then decide which issues will be discussed at your next Stepfamily Meeting. If you have to table an issue, explain why and tell the kids when it will be addressed. In the end, strive to come up with a list of common House Rules, roles and responsibilities which meet everyone's needs.

If they worked well in the past, existing or previous family structures can be a good starting point. In fact, avoid overhauling or dismantling existing House Rules. This will only lead to confusion and resentment. Instead, take things one day—and one Stepfamily Meeting—at a time. Come together, as a couple, and agree on what makes the most sense or is most important to ensuring the functioning, welfare and safety of each member of your stepfamily.

Step 1: Decide on Must-Have House Rules

When our families function well, other aspects of our lives tend to run more smoothly. By actively making your stepfamily a place in which everyone feels secure, understood and supported, you and your partner help ensure the future success of your couple's relationship and your stepfamily relationships. You do that by communicating that your stepfamily is capable of functioning as a team that's united through shared House Rules, responsibilities and rewards. It's up to you two to set the tone for mutual respect, consideration, concern and cooperation.

Your list of absolute, must-have House Rules and boundaries should take into consideration what's going on now and what you both envision for your stepfamily's future. By making sure they sync up with your values and beliefs, you'll be one step closer to meeting your individual and family goals. Without a shared history, however, identifying shared goals you can both hang your hats on can be challenging. This is especially true early on, when you're likely to be very busy putting out fires or simply learning to coexist.

This makes setting House Rules and establishing clear roles within your shared home particularly important, whether you all live together full-time or not. That's because a solid foundation everyone can rely on, work from and contribute to creates a sense of belonging in your home. It also communicates concern for everyone's well-being and helps your household run more smoothly, taking shape as realistic and achievable expectations.

House Rules themselves are meant to address everyday concerns and to help children learn lifelong lessons; ones you hope to pass onto them and ones which reflect your stepfamily's collective values. Each person's idea of what those are differs, so it's important to know which lessons both you and your partner find it necessary to impart. Consider this your joint "must-haves" list. First, write out separate lists: You write one and your partner writes one. Now, share your results. Look for areas of common concern. Circle those. Then go back, noticing any differences.

Your list of concerns may range from curfew times to table manners. They may vary based on differences in the ages of your stepchildren and, if you have any, children. One of you may be more concerned about bedtimes, while the other is focused on chores getting done. Considered as a whole, decide which sorts of rules would truly make your home run more safely and effectively. This is a good time to refer back to the Appendix, revisiting the questions I've included which are meant to get you and your partner thinking more deeply about this topic [see "Arriving at Must-Have House Rules: What does stepfamily life look like to you—the (step-)parents?"].

As you review the lists you've just created, discuss your individual reasons for wanting to establish related House Rules. A common concern, for parents and stepparents, is a desire to create order while reducing chaos in the home. No matter what, resist judging one another's list items and supporting rationales as "right" or "wrong." If your viewpoints or values differ, express curiosity and make time to understand where the other partner is coming from. In the end, you want to arrive at a list of mutual concerns you agree on. If this is difficult, set the exercise aside for a few days.

Getting clear about what each of you envision for your stepfamily and which House Rules will help you achieve that will get you on the same page. It will also help you communicate their importance to the children, who you'll then be better equipped to tell: What's expected of them, why that's important and what will happen if the rules are broken. In life, we all face consequences in connection with our actions or our failure to act. Teaching them to be responsible and face consequences now is an act of kindness that keeps them from being blindsided in the future.

Another good reason for establishing House Rules is that it's your responsibility, as a parent and/or stepparent, to ensure the children's safety and well-being. It may not always be fun, but it's what you signed up for when you and your partner made a commitment to one another. Children, in fact, thrive when household boundaries are clear and consistent. And, trust me: If you don't lead them to guiding values in the home, they'll learn them elsewhere. So, be accountable yourselves. Set rules which are there to protect them and will help them become responsible, fully-functioning and independent adults.

Step 2: Make Your Rules & Consequences Clear

Without rules or consequences in place, life is infinitely more difficult. Think of a time you experienced conflict over a need to negotiate a situation that was left open to interpretation. It's not much fun, is it? Boundaries and rules make life easier for everyone, especially when you set them in advance. As children grow, so do the number of issues which need to be addressed through House Rules. Prior planning can help you avoid future problems. Yet, there's hope no matter where you are in the process. As you and your partner work together to set rules and consequences for your stepfamily home, remember that without them life can quickly spiral out of control.

By investing the energy now, you'll reap the benefits more quickly! Refer back to your earlier conversation and individual lists. Using what you learned from one another, while discussing your individual concerns, draft a new list. This joint "must-haves" list should address what you both feel are your family's most pressing needs. Knowing what is and isn't acceptable then gives you a roadmap for getting your stepfamily where you both want it to be. This couple's list will help you set clear rules and consequences you can confidently communicate to the children.

Aim to set reasonable limits which give those children the freedom to stretch to the edge of your stepfamily's boundaries without going beyond them. The older the children, the greater their need to individuate and experience themselves as real contributors in the home. This is part of the developmental process, particularly for teens. Under those circumstances, knowing where their autonomy ends and your authority begins will be comforting and enlightening. It'll also give you two increased peace of mind.

If you've been lax about enforcing rules in the past, begin with those which are already established and familiar. That gives everyone a chance to ease into getting back on track and to adapt to a potentially new process whereby you, the stepmother, is also to be respected as an enforcer of the household rules. And, as Papernow said, make sure the parent is the disciplinarian. If they're your kids, that's you. If they're your husband's, that's him. If it wasn't already communicated, now is also a good time to clarify your roles to one another and to the children: "We're both here to enforce the rules," he might say, "but I'll be the one dishing out the final punishment." Or something like it.

I realize that stepparents are sometimes reluctant to or discouraged from providing structure and enforcing limits. Well, my view is this: Once you and your partner have established a set of rules and attached consequences for breaking them, you aren't overstepping anything at all. You're merely following through on a plan you put in place together. While it may take several attempts to arrive at a full list of rules and consequences you both agree on as being important in your stepfamily, you'll get there. In the meantime, prioritize and implement them as you go.

For clarity's sake, always consider the children's ages. Rules for young children should be simple and specific. As needed, be prepared to spell things out (literally, in list form) and to offer gentle reminders until they incorporate them as habit. Limit the number of rules you set for them, starting off with no more than five. Again, prioritize. Focus on those rules which will be the most beneficial to any youngsters in your home. As they begin to modify their behaviors around them, add a few more—but not so many that they become discouraged or want to give up.

Consider putting a reward system in place, too, especially with this younger age group. People of all ages often do things because they're motivated or otherwise incented to do them. Rewards can certainly include things like charts or calendars which get checkmarks or gold stars anytime the child completes an assigned chore. This is a good visual tool, giving them a peek at the progress they've made. Most of us also like knowing that what we did made us or someone close to us happy, so consider rewarding them with: small change, happy face stickers or a personal note of thanks from you or their father. That alone may motivate the kids to do what's asked of them.

Rules for older kids don't need to be quite so specific, though the success of this particular strategy may vary by child. Adolescents and teens benefit from fewer hard-and-fast rules and a greater ability to guide their own conduct. Teens, in general, tend to view rules as something to be avoided. Instead, have them participate in creating rules for fair conduct. The more ownership they take over this activity, as I've said, the more likely it is they'll respect those guidelines. Try to involve them in setting consequences of their own versus push for standards you've set for them.

Enforcing House Rules does require having consequences in place for when they're broken and these must be age-based, as well. To really have an impact, it's best if a consequence holds importance for the person who broke the rule. Let's say three of your stepchildren break the same rule, neglecting to do their homework. TV privileges may be important to the youngest, internet access to the adolescent and going out with friends to the oldest. The consequences of their actions need to be relative to them, credible for the situation and attention-grabbing.

Broad rules (i.e., "We always tell the truth") can also be applied and work well with any age group, including adults. This drives home the fact that it's not okay to say one thing and do another. Children learn the most by observing what we, their parents and/or stepparents, do. You're at your most influential when you do what it is you say is important to you. Showing the kids that even we need to follow House Rules will help them accept their own consequences more easily. After all, everyone can benefit by learning from their mistakes.

Step 3: Communicate & Live by Those Rules

Learning to live by your House Rules will make home life more pleasant for everyone. Yet, truly understanding what's expected of us begins with open and honest communication. I can't stress that enough and speak from experience when I say that, especially for a child, confusing House Rules or boundaries can be nearly as detrimental as non-existent House Rules or boundaries. The same principle applies to their enforcement and related consequences. As it would be in any family, the first step is to discuss the matter privately with your partner.

Using your "must-haves" list, come to a consensus and create a unified front before trying to enforce rules and apply consequences for the children—who need to know that you're working together and plan on staying together no matter what. And, trust me, they'll test you! In the Appendix, you'll find a list of conversation starters you and your partner can use to create House Rules which make sense for your stepfamily. Use them in your Stepfamily Meeting, too, to encourage acceptance and age-appropriate input (see "Stepfamily House Rule Conversation Starters").

The goal is get all of you thinking more deeply about everyone's comfort and safety levels. Just as you did earlier, start with those topics which make the most sense given your unique situation. Set aside quiet time in which you and your partner discuss them. Avoid analyzing and instead respond based on what it is you'd like to see happen in your home. Once you've decided which particular areas matter most and what you'll do about them, acknowledge one another for your participation.

When it comes time to share what you've decided with the children, schedule a Stepfamily Meeting. Be sure everyone can be present and minimize distractions: Turn off radios, TVs, smartphones, etc. Make it clear that your initial meeting will be limited to one hour. (By letting everyone know upfront that it won't go on forever, you'll enjoy better participation.) In advance, explain the reason for the meeting and/or create an agenda, asking anyone who has an issue they'd like to discuss to contribute to it. Older kids may have specific needs they want your House Rules to address. If so, listen to what they have to say.

Hold your meeting in a neutral place that isn't too formal or fussy. For your stepfamily, that may be the dining room table or the living room couch. Make it comfortable and enjoyable but do limit distractions. Let the dog out to "do his business" ahead of time, have the kids tell their friends they won't be able to answer the phone/door, etc. When you begin, start by having everyone briefly state what it is they hope to learn. (It may be helpful to take notes!)

Then, explain the reason behind your House Rules. Let the kids know that both of you came to an agreement on the rules you're about to cover and that either of you is authorized to enforce them *without* question. Be clear that not responding to a stepparent who tries to enforce a rule means the child is, in fact, breaking a House Rule. Be sure the children also understand what will happen if they break any given rule you two have set for your home. Provide nonspecific examples, illustrating that there will be immediate consequences which they may not like very much.

Let them know what role they play in upholding your stepfamily's House Rules responsibly. Make it *clear* that they have a choice: They are free to either follow the rules or face the consequences. The decision is theirs. Above all, be sure they know that it's their responsibility to follow the rules. The biological parent should take the lead on this and drive home the fact that following through with uncomfortable consequences will result from choices *they* make.

It won't take long for this equation to sink in. Even the youngest members of your household will learn quickly that actions have consequences. It may be painful, at first, to follow through. It's particularly painful for parents who are used to "saving" their children from perceived pain or suffering. In reality, though, this saves them from nothing. If anything, it delays their ability to develop patterns of responsible behavior which will come in handy in the future. That said, know that the rules you set now won't necessarily stay in place forever. In fact, I know they won't.

As children grow and new issues crop up, you and your partner will need to establish new or different sets of rules to accommodate for your family's change in circumstances. Too, while there is no limit to the number of rules you set for your home, the underlying principle must remain the same: Your stepfamily's rules should reflect the values you and your spouse hold dear and the lessons you wish to impart to the children. Let that be your focus. Also, with too many rules in place, you risk complicating things and making it impossible for the children to comply.

Finally, the best way to help remind everyone about House Rules and responsibilities is to have them posted where they can be clearly seen and referenced. For my clients, a popular location is the fridge door. When it comes to House Rules, list them in order of priority and write them in a way that's succinct and legible to all. When it comes to chore lists, posting customized daily or weekly lists on the kids' bedroom doors is helpful. Starting at age five or six, they can help create those lists and add some personal flair which helps drive home the concept of ownership.

One surefire way to ensure widespread accountability is to follow the House Rules yourselves. You can't ask a child to do something if you're not willing to it yourself. Teach them what *is* and *isn't* acceptable through modeling.

A Few Final Words on House Rules, etc.

If you just moved into your stepfamily home, don't expect—or attempt—to change things overnight or too soon.

"Moving prematurely into (the role) of limit setter is a recipe for disaster," Papernow cautioned, "especially with adolescent stepkids. Stepmothers do often have a lot of perspective about how kids can use more limits. However, parents have a lot of perspective about who their kids are, what they're accustomed to and what their emotional needs are."

"In my experience," she added, "what kids actually need lies somewhere between the stepparent's (concept) of limits and the parent's. When this goes well, stepparents can help parents 'firm up' and parents can help stepparents 'warm up.' Again, parents have to do the actual limit setting until stepparents have *really* trusting relationships with their stepkids."

When change occurs slowly, the results are both better and longer lasting. In addition, keep modeling and reflecting the sorts of values and behaviors you'd like to see instilled in your home. When it comes to communicating, be specific about what you hope for, so others aren't guessing what it is you're thinking or need from them.

Parents must take an active role in this, as well, by modeling and eventually explaining what it is you're all expected to do and why. One way your partner can do that is by staying seated during dinner. If Dad keeps getting up to do this or that (Check your cell phone much?), the children will believe they can do the same. Have everything you need to enjoy a meal together on the table, so there's no need—beyond bathroom breaks—for anyone to get up in the middle of it. Observe, too, how often you text when the stepkids are with you. Are you setting a good example? Know, too, that changes in stepfamily dynamics impact children's perspectives and behaviors in a big way.

"As the rate and amount of change go up," Papernow said, "child well-being goes down. So, the unhappy truth is, what may make Stepmom comfortable may be asking a lot of stepkids. That doesn't mean Stepmom shouldn't ask. It's just that stepmoms must understand that, if they want (to shift the) boundaries in their new families, they're *asking* something of kids which may be hard for them. And may be just a bit too much change for some of them."

Old habits die hard. This is true for all of us. Accept the fact that it may take your stepkids quite a while to adjust to new House Rules, roles and responsibilities. Have compassion and empathy for what they're going through, so you'll be better positioned to resist viewing behaviors you find off-putting or irritating as somehow ill-intended. Remind yourself that Rome wasn't built in a day. It took decades to construct that Empire.

"It's one thing to say, 'Hey! I'd really appreciate it if you could ____'," Papernow noted. "It's an entirely different thing to say, 'Pick up your backpacks and put them away or there will be consequences.' What feels messy or intrusive to a stepmother may feel normal and family-like to her stepkids and their father. Stepmom will be much more successful if she can treat this as a cultural difference and not as an issue of right and wrong."

"If Dad says, 'But that's the way they've always done it,' don't infer that he's (siding with them) out of guilt. He may be—but he may also be communicating something important about his kids. It would certainly be nice for Stepmom if Dad also said, 'I hear this is tough for you. Let's talk about it.' Yet, coming across as rather righteous doesn't tend to open the doors of most partners' hearts. It is *very* hard to walk into a foreign culture, as a stranger in a strange land, but solving your stepfamily's problems by 'setting firm boundaries' will make a terrible mess."

While you're members of the same stepfamily, each of your roles is distinct. Let Dad be the disciplinarian. Focus on enforcing rules and boundaries with compassion in your heart. As needed, be firm about what's important to you but don't resist accepting new information which can help you fill your role successfully. Instead, as a couple, bring everyone together to achieve common goals which honor your differences and are based in empathy and concern.

There's no right or wrong. There's only what's best for your individual stepfamily.

CHAPTER 13

Your Stepfamily's Approach to Kickback

Parenting usually involves taking on a primary disciplinary role within the home. It's no different in stepfamilies, though stepparents—with the exception of when they're parenting their own children—are strongly advised to and typically step down from a power position. Instead, they provide support by enforcing the rules of the home. This is important to remember when considering your stepfamily's approach to consequences and any potential kickback.

Take your time with this topic, especially if older children (i.e., teens) are involved. The biological parent should remain the primary disciplinarian. This is *crucial* during the early stages of your stepfamily's development. For example, when both the biological parent and the stepparent are present, discipline is best administered by the biological parent. Children need time to adjust to having a stepparent in the mix and may never view him or her as having the authority to discipline them. This has nothing to do with you or your efforts. It's a given that they'd turn to their own parents for guidance; they've come to learn and understand that that's who's responsible for them.

When the biological parent is absent from the home, or whatever situation you find yourself in, it's best to approach any behaviors which you and your partner have determined to be inappropriate as if your role is closer to that of another adult providing supervision. We've discussed this: Consider yourself to be someone along the lines of a teacher, a visiting relative, etc. You're the one in charge but you're *not* their parent. Your authority to enforce the rules of the home should have been communicated to the children already, by your partner. If not, make sure he makes time to immediately clarify for them that you have his blessing and the ability to carry out his wishes.

As the children grow to trust and understand your position within the home, they may eventually become more comfortable with the idea of you being some sort of disciplinarian to them. Yet, you and your partner should always take your cues from the children. Let them lead you versus try to force what will no doubt feel like unnatural parental authority on them. If you don't, you risk adding to their confusion and stirring up resentment in your relationships with them. Loyalty binds, in and of themselves, can stir up feelings of uncertainty. In other words, do they listen to and take direction from you ... or their parent?

Through gentle conversation, you and your partner can certainly help the children understand that, just as a parent can have two or more children and share unique relationships with each of them, a child can have two or more "parents" (or adult figures) in their life and share unique relationships with each of them. What's most important is developing a relationship with your stepchild which feels authentic, is mutually respectful and helps you trust one another gradually over an extended period of time.

Why Just Saying "No!" Won't Work

Here's something I bet you can relate to. When I was a kid, if one of my parents told me, "No!" I'd ask (in a tiny, whiny, itty-bitty voice): "But, whyyyy???!!!" Their go-to response? "Because I said so, that's why!" That doesn't work. It didn't work for me. It didn't work with my own son. And it didn't work with either of my stepdaughters. I know for sure that it won't work with your kids or stepkids, either. But, really, why is that?

"No" is not enough. While it never has been, children today have the potential to be way savvier than we were. They not only have books at their disposal; they also have access to the internet. They read, they watch YouTube videos, they hop on Reddit and use Snap Chat or Instagram to ask questions of their peers. Thanks to social media, they can generate opinions from hundreds of their peers around the world in a matter of minutes; in seconds, really. If that fails? They can hop on Google, Bing or another search engine and look up just about any topic imaginable.

Like your younger self, they want and deserve a better answer than, "Because I said so!" Of course, if he or she is about to run across a busy street, yell, "No!" at the top of your lungs. In that case, there's no time to address: "Why not?" But that's not what we're talking about here and few situations leave little time for nothing more than a glib reply. Imagine, for a moment, that your teenage stepdaughter comes down the stairs wearing a skirt that's so short you wonder if the Aerie factory ran out of fabric while making it.

She's headed out the door to catch the school bus when you catch a glimpse at her hemline or, even worse, her underwear. You stop what you're doing, head over to where she is and tell her that under no circumstance is she to consider this to be appropriate school attire. Whether she's eight or eighteen is irrelevant. She then turns around and asks you, "Why not?" If you simply told her, "Because I *said* so!" it's unlikely she'd happily head back upstairs and say, "Okay, sure!" Most probably she'd roll her eyes at you and then head straight out the door.

What can you say, instead, that will truly get to the root of the problem? You could begin, "Taylor, we've talked about what's okay and what's not okay to wear to school." Hopefully you and her parent did, in fact, do this prior to the issue coming up at all. You continue: "There's a school dress code. All students need to abide by it. There's also a family dress code and you need to abide by that, too. If you want, I'm happy to review those details with you now, as you go back upstairs to change. Would you like my help choosing something else?"

A few things may happen next:

- She may try to stall, so you'll run late and let her go.
- She may say, "You're *not* my mom. I'll wear what I want!"
- She may storm upstairs, knowing you're right about all of it.
- She may say, "I have *nothing* to wear." (You: "Let's find something.")

I say these things not to scare you but to prepare you. The best defense to any child's objection is a firm but caring offensive strategy. This is where having clear, concise and communicated House Rules comes in handy. It's also a good time to reflect back on any discussions you and your partner have had about what is and isn't considered acceptable in your home—and what you're both prepared to do to remedy situations like this one.

What to Do When They Talk Back

You can never truly predict what your stepchildren will do or say. That's true of any child. However, you can set some guidelines and ground rules for how you'll interpret what they do and say. You can even prepare yourself, in advance, for dealing with their kickback, comebacks and any fallout that arises around a given situation.

Stall tactics are one way children (and, yes, immature adults) go about trying to get their own way. Those children are smart enough to know that, as responsible adults, you and your partner don't like showing up late for work or for any other commitments you have either inside or outside the home. It's as if they're saying, "I know you hate being late or seeing me get to school late, so I'm gonna try this strategy and hope to get what it is I want out of it." They view delay strategies as a way to regain control over the situation and, thereby, you.

If you give in, you're essentially telling them they're not important enough to waste your time on. I mean, let's face facts: Enforcing boundaries does take time and energy. Yet, you, your partner and the school have set certain boundaries for a reason. Ideally, that's to ensure the overall health and development of your (step-)children. That alone is worth the time and energy it takes to enforce them. The consequence, for you, is a loss of a few minutes. In the grand scheme of things, it's a worthwhile investment.

As for, "You're *not* my mom (or dad)," the best response is: "You're right. I'm not. But I am responsible for your safety and well-being. And those things matter to me. You matter to me." Offer to talk with them about the situation later in the day, when their biological parent can also be present. As you do that, guide them to the behavior you want to see them demonstrate. For even better results, set a time when you can all: Sit down, give the topic some consideration and agree to a policy going forward.

By acknowledging that what your stepchild said is correct, you've diffused the situation. By being willing to talk it out later and to set a time in which you can do that, you're demonstrating a willingness to hear what she has to say. You've also modeled mature behavior by being open to a discussion about her concerns. Lastly, you've reinforced the topic of child welfare while setting a boundary that says, "I can't talk about this now—but I *will* make time for you. I promise." Just be sure to follow through.

It's natural and healthy for children, including teens, to test our boundaries. Part of the growing process, for them, involves figuring out: Where do you end and where do I begin? It doesn't matter if you're their parent or their stepparent. The end goal is the same, as far as they're concerned. They want to test the waters but look to us—once they've learned to trust and respect us—to reel them back in when the boundaries they're crossing have the potential to cause them harm.

And, whatever they say, keep the fence around your heart open as you focus on their safety and security.

CHAPTER 14

What Stepfamily Boundaries Won't Do for You

U p to this point, you've learned what boundaries are and aren't. You've learned how to set them, what to base them on so they'll be truly effective and which roles you and your partner play in communicating and enforcing them. You've also learned that there's no right or wrong way to do any of that. Rather, there's what works (or doesn't) within your individual stepfamily. Still, I hear you saying: "What about the *other* house?! Their mom lets them do whatever they want. How do we get past that? Are we supposed to sit by and watch the chaos unfold?"

This can be a major concern for stepfamilies everywhere. Families which form as a result of divorce generally wind up navigating different viewpoints, disparate House Rules and boundary issues which seem daunting at best. Nowhere is this felt as strongly as when it comes to boundaries, because what one parent or family believes is inappropriate may seem totally acceptable to another. Any stepmom who's ever suffered through a bout of midnight texts from the ex can attest to this. Yet, here's the thing: We *can't* control the other home.

You wouldn't want anyone controlling what goes on in yours, right? The best way to deal with discrepancies like these is to remember what you do have control over. You and your spouse, or partner, are in charge of guarding the gate that either blocks or gives others entry to your literal and figurative stepfamily abode. It's up to you two to decide who or what is granted access. That's true for individuals, behaviors, routines, habits, etc. What happens once you're all inside the home is (to a certain degree) within your control. What happens outside of it? Is not.

Think back to your own childhood. Your parents probably ran their household differently than you and your partner now run yours. This is also true of the workplace. Unless you're the CEO, you have little say in or control over: how it functions, which practices are deemed acceptable and what policies are put in place to encourage them. The same goes for schools, churches and group settings of all kinds. You can only supervise and be responsible for what's rightfully yours to oversee. As a result, there's no point stressing out over what you simply can't control.

So, view the situation as inevitable. Accept the fact that you can't micromanage what goes on at every moment of your children's and/or stepchildren's lives. Instead, focus your attention on learning to recognize and control your reactions to what's going on. This will then help you pick your battles wisely and keep things in perspective, especially when it comes to the other home.

Pick Your Battles Wisely

Every home, institution, public space and community has its own set of rules and boundaries. Some are implicit, as in it's not okay to park your boat or RV on your neighbor's lawn. Others are explicit: "No Swimming Without a Lifeguard on Duty!" Each reflects a set of values and beliefs which is tied to a sort of mission statement or life's ambition. All result in codes of conduct and legacies of norms for behavior which are understood to be acceptable and expected in that particular domain. The gate is heavily guarded and the fee for entry is compliance.

It only makes sense, then, that exes' homes would operate differently from our own. After all, if that person was so likeminded, why divorce them in the first place? Accept their values and beliefs as their own. So what if yours are different? Heck, your current partner's may differ wildly from yours. The difference is that you two are on a mission to meet somewhere in the middle and reach a compromise everyone in your stepfamily can live with. Expecting either of your exes' views to be similar to or the same as yours is unrealistic. It'll drive you crazy, if you let it.

What you *can* do to encourage peace and harmony within your own stepfamily home, particularly as it relates to your stepkids, is to look for common ground. I'll admit that creating boundaries everyone will agree to can be difficult. That's where building on what's already in place comes into play, helping ease the kids' transition between homes and minimizing any friction or kickback you might otherwise be subject to by calling for an overhaul. Think of this as picking your battles wisely. Better yet, resist thinking in terms of battlegrounds and territories.

Not everything about stepfamily life needs to result in a battle for power or control. Similarly, not every battle is yours to fight or win. Some are just plain *not* worth the hassle. If not straightening up their bedrooms or mowing the grass before it gets too long are common complaints you lob at your partner about his kids' lack of accountability, ask who's truly being hurt in the process. Chances are you may be the only one feeling the weight of that complaint.

By contrast, some battles *are* worth engaging in: It's worth standing firm on topics like being respectful of those around us, being responsible for our actions and demonstrating behaviors which sync up with our stepfamily's core values. This is especially true if you've invested time and energy setting deliberate boundaries which are intended to keep everyone in your stepfamily healthy, strong and safe from harm. The more they're rooted in your shared beliefs, the clearer and better defined your boundaries will be. They'll also be easier to communicate, enforce and negotiate.

In their landmark book for the Harvard Negotiation Project, *Getting to Yes: Negotiating Agreement without Giving in*, Roger Fisher, LLB, and William Ury, PhD, noted that it's more important to focus on interests than on positions. That is, when dealing with any sort of problem, make time to separate the person from the issue at hand. If your stepson hasn't done the mowing, as he's supposed to, don't jump to assuming the worst. Avoid telling your partner, "Your son is so lazy!" and don't admonish your stepson with, "Why can't you do this *one* chore on time?"

Doing so immediately pushes others into defense mode, pushing the possibility for any sort of productive negotiation or communication into a Failure Zone. In order to be successful at getting what you want or need, consider what's at stake. The higher the stakes, the higher the need to step back and look at the big picture before you react. By honing your negotiation skills, you'll be better able to get everyone on the same page and to help them see the value and benefit of embracing your stepfamily's boundaries versus bristle at the mere thought of them.

Your goal *is* to get everyone on board, correct? Well, the quickest way to do that is to stop taking a righteous approach. Stop placing blame, stop complaining and stop thinking you're the only one who knows right from wrong. Give up the need to defend your position and forget trying to sway everyone else to your way of thinking.

Yours is not the only way. Now, it can be a challenge to accept that another person's perspective may lead to acceptable outcomes, especially when that person is a stepkid or an ex-spouse who's typically aggressive toward you.

This makes it doubly important to know what your boundaries are around verbal, emotional and physical aggression or violence. Be sure they're firmly in place, well-communicated and understood by all before you dig into any contentious topic. Those boundaries, however, shouldn't keep you from being able to listen to what the other person has to say. What they should do is help you put ground rules in place which lead to productive conversations marked by civil interactions and well-chosen words.

I suggest that your couple's ground rules for your stepfamily include:

- Private matters are to be kept private.
- Respectful, dignified interaction is a must.
- Verbal and/or physical threats won't be tolerated.
- Yelling, screaming, swearing and taunting are forbidden.
- Whining or complaining to third parties (aka Mom) is not okay.

Add whatever you feel is important when it comes to being able to authentically pay attention to and hear one another's perspectives. None of this will be easy. Nor will it be simple. Yet, in order to be sure your boundaries are respected, you need to start somewhere. Without guidelines in place for discussing and negotiating what you know to be difficult or combative topics for your stepfamily, it will be impossible to make any real progress on an issue.

When exes are involved in these conversations and things do not go well, the logical next step often takes the form of litigation. We're talking here about discussions related to visitation, holiday schedules, custody splits and the like. Litigation should be a last resort, as it can be costly and may result in you and your partner having even less of a say in (and, thereby, less control over) any remedies which are reached by outside parties such as lawyers or courts of law. That wouldn't be a win-win situation at all. It'd be more of a lose-lose scenario.

There may even be times when the person you need to negotiate with is your partner. Since this is someone you're deeply committed to, the negotiations must go well. Again, you'd be wise to listen more than you talk and to resist defending a position the other simply can't get behind. For example, Bernard and I had been together roughly six months when we were driving home after a dinner party held at his parents' place. Like most new couples, we'd previously had plenty of conversations about our likes, our dislikes, our emotional sore spots. That sort of stuff.

While discussing the evening and the fun we had, I affectionately called him "my little piggy." This was in reference to both his general appetite and his love of desserts. All of a sudden, his face took on an expression I'd never seen before. In a fit of anger, he looked at me and said, "Don't you *ever* call me that again, understand?!" I was shocked, taken aback by his reaction. I was at a total loss, in fact. He refused to talk about it further, so I let it go. Still, tears rolled down my face. When we got home, I began defending my position once again.

We went back and forth. I explained that I thought the nickname was "funny and cute"—like him! He explained that he felt I was being disrespectful toward him. I told him that, in the home I grew up in, it was a term of endearment. I then questioned his thought process. This only made matters worse. Reasoning with him about what I viewed as an overreaction to a "harmless" pet name wasn't getting us anywhere. For Bernard, the moniker was simply offensive.

He took it to mean that I found his behavior at the party inappropriate, as if I were saying he had gorged himself in front of others. My words had touched a wound deep inside him. Had I insisted that I didn't mean any harm and he should just "get over it," we might not be together today. He had a boundary and I had crossed it. Whether or not I could relate, hearing him out and respecting his viewpoint was a small price to pay for what's become a lifelong partnership in which we express ourselves authentically and find common ground despite our differences.

While it's an uncommon example, I'm sure you and your partner share differences of your own. If something can be done to resolve even one of them, do what it takes to reach a compromise. On any issues you can't reach an agreement on, agree to disagree—but do so lovingly versus spitefully or resentfully. Your relationship is the cornerstone of your stepfamily, so all other successes stem from your willingness and ability to reach an intimate understanding of one another's needs. Once you two are in agreement, everything else will fall in place more easily.

Keep Things in Perspective

Without being able to control what goes on in their other parents' homes, how can you possibly expect to get a hefty return on the investment you and your partner are now making to set and enforce reliable boundaries for the kids? Good question!

Coaching clients often tell me, "Yeah, I'm doing all this work to make our home safe for them. We've established clear rules and boundaries. Then they go back to Mom's only to be told they can do whatever they please. So, what's the point, if they don't have rules or responsibilities—or face consequences—in the other home?"

To say the least, these (step-)parents feel frustrated. You might, too. Here you are doing all you can to learn about boundary setting, to figure out what your role is in all of this and to work with your partner to reach agreements about things the other home seems to care less about. You've done all you can to ensure that your stepfamily House Rules and boundaries are respected. You and your partner have been clear and specific in your talks with the children. You may have begged or pleaded for compliance. You may have even tried bargaining ... to no avail.

Your stepkids simply won't abide by your boundaries and you're pretty sure it's because whatever's going on in the other home is affecting how they feel about what's expected of them in your stepfamily home. One strategy I'd like you to try is to always keep things in perspective. In a prior chapter, we talked about Rome not being built in a day. The same is true for the safety net that is the imaginary, gated fence encircling your stepfamily. It takes a lot of work to go from not having a fence in place at all to having a darling one with an operative gate standing firm around you.

Time is on your side, particularly if you and your partner are committed to addressing the issues of House Rules and boundaries as a team. The more opportunities you have to reinforce positive behaviors and to model appropriate interactions in your home, the closer you'll be to achieving the goal of getting the kids to stand behind any rules and boundaries you've set. Just remember to keep enforcing them and resist giving up or giving in. Here, I want to share with you a few more ways you can go about getting children to respect any decisions you've made for your home.

In order for true and lasting change to occur, we need to avoid tactics of coercion. We need to stop trying to change other people and their viewpoints. Instead, we need to begin looking for patterns in existing or emerging behaviors which support the boundaries we're hoping to instill—and reward those! When your stepdaughter or stepson does something in line with a stepfamily boundary, make their accomplishment a teachable moment. Show gratitude for their behavior and explain how what they did aligns with the reasoning behind your House Rules and boundaries.

Catch them in the act of upholding them and say something meaningful:

- "Hannah, I'm really proud of the way you cleaned up your room. It looks lovely when your clothes are put away and your bed is made. I really value the effort you put into making the house look so nice."
- "Junior, thanks for making a difference by clearing out the garage and putting everyone's bikes away so neatly. It's a lot safer to move around in there, especially for your little brother. Good thinking!"
- "Lucy, it was great to come out of the kitchen and see that the table was already set. Thanks for doing that in time for dinner. It was great enjoying a hot meal together. You made that happen!"
- "Mason, it was really smart of you to wash and put away your sports gear after practice. It's nice knowing that it'll be ready for you the next time you need it. Great job!"

While at George Mason University, I studied conflict resolution, communication and family dynamics. That's when I learned that conflict need not be avoided but seen as an opportunity to learn about the other person's viewpoints and perspectives. During my time there, I was also introduced to the bestselling book *Difficult Conversations: How to Discuss What Matters Most*, written by Douglas Stone, JD, Bruce Patton, JD, and Sheila Heen, JD. Their strategies helped me understand what was really going on with the ex, my stepdaughters and even my son.

As a result, I became increasingly curious about what the real issue was behind any conflict we were experiencing and less concerned with defending my own positions. Being involved in relationships (yes, even ones we didn't necessarily ask for or anticipate) requires understanding the wants and needs of others, as well as our own. As long as you work to keep a dialogue going, there will always be the possibility that you might one day come to an agreement and break through any impasse that keeps insufficient or ineffective boundaries in place.

The bottom line in all of this is getting everyone's needs met. Once we know what those are, we have room to negotiate with one another. Yet, what if the other person refuses to let go of their own position, wants nothing to do with you or is determined to "not let you win"—what then? Well, there are still many respectful and dignified ways to cope with the situation. This is true whether it's you or your partner who's come up against resistance from them.

- First, acknowledge what you heard. This validates the other person's humanness. You don't have to agree with (or like) them or their opinions. You simply need to validate that you heard what they said to you.
- Next, calmly and firmly recap what your position is and why you feel the way you do. Keep it brief.
- Third, share what you plan to do about the problem. Explain what steps you'll take, making sure you're willing and ready to act on them. Don't offer up empty threats. In fact, don't threaten in any way.
- Finally, earning respect requires saying what you mean and walking the talk: It's time to take action.

Of those four steps, the last one might be the hardest to fulfill. It's easy to say you'll "take the car keys away" the next time your stepson comes home drunk or high. It's another to actually do it. It takes courage to act on those words, especially if you're likely to face blowback from your stepson, the other biological parent, etc.

This is where clear, upfront communication about your House Rules and boundaries and a united front come in handy. You and your partner must be in agreement on issues like these well before they become problematic. In addition, you'd be wise to align yourself with a support group, a counselor and/or a friend who will have your back and understand the reasoning behind your decisions. (It's easier to stand your ground when others hold you up.)

If you or your partner begin to waver, ask yourselves: "How would we feel if we woke up tomorrow and the behavior we forbade—but failed to correct—caused irreversible harm?" In other words, how would you feel if your stepson injured someone while he was inebriated? Or his younger siblings decided to get drunk or high, since their brother got away with it? Could you live with that? Regret is a terrible feeling and can eat at you over the course of a lifetime, so never compromise your stepfamily values and beliefs for a momentary respite from the kids' complaints.

As a couple, remember that the one thing you can control is what goes on in your home. Make it a point to arrive at decisions you can firmly stand behind and then quickly follow through on for the safety, security and well-being of everyone within it. Start by turning to the Appendix, where you'll find the "Our Boundaries, Defined" worksheet. Along with everything else you've learned here, my hope is that it sets you on a path that's paved with healthier boundaries, more enforceable House Rules and a stepfamily experience that finds you living your own personally crafted version of the white-picket-fence dream.

Setting boundaries won't fix your problems overnight. It will, however, give you the courage to go the distance!

CHAPTER 15

A Personal Note from Claudette

O n Jan 31, 1990, I met a wonderful man who would rock my world in a number of ways. I'd been looking for a partner to share my life with. Not someone who'd do everything for me or barely be there—but someone to share my life's journey with. On our first date together, Bernard and I talked until 4 a.m. Despite that long talk and the others which followed, I hadn't spent much time considering the impact his two young daughters (then ages six and seven) would also have on our relationship. Instead, I figured they'd be great sisters to my own son who was close in age.

You see, I'd grown up adoring Julie Andrews in *The Sound of Music* and watching *The Brady Bunch* on TV. Maybe you did, too. They made it look so simple! You get married, bring the kids home and sing "Do Rei Me" or "It's a Sunshine Day" in harmony. Yet, when our "new" family gave it a go, something strange happened. There were too many false notes. Both the song and the script fell apart. Nothing went according to melody. Nothing at all. Everyone and everything was a jumbled, off-key mess. What was I doing wrong?!

I couldn't get along with anyone in my husband's extended family, either, and felt every bit the outsider. I'd lost control over my life and my home. Bernard and I were constantly at odds about how we should raise our kids. We quickly became adversaries divided along biological fault lines. There were no real boundaries in our home. I didn't know where I ended and anyone else began outside of my son, Sebastien. Bernard's kids and family suddenly seemed to be way more important to him than I was. I no longer felt like his No. 1. My sense of identity withered and my self-esteem shrunk right alongside it. I also became highly frustrated.

Is this story starting to sound familiar? If you're in a stepfamily, I don't doubt it! Pent-up anger molded a new identity for me. I became depressed, felt lost and eventually hit rock bottom. My husband tried to help. But, rather than part of the solution, I viewed him as the root of our problems. His need to put his daughters and other family concerns first *made* me this way! So I thought, until a conversation with a therapist changed my perspective and our stepfamily trajectory forever. Asked what I'd love to do if I weren't sitting there in counseling—or battling my demons at home—I said I'd go back to school to become a psychologist.

The therapist then asked, gently, "What's holding you back?" I nearly blurted out, "Bernard!" But, the truth was, my own fear of failure and I were the real culprits. Deep down, I knew it. With lots of encouragement and support from both my therapist and my husband, I went back to school at age 36. Nine years later I graduated with the highest honors possible and a degree from George Mason University. That turning point was pivotal in helping me see how I could bridge the gap between my desire to be a positive role model in our kids' lives and my yearning to enjoy an identity and some real value of my own.

I'd finally found my place in the world, both in our stepfamily and in the relationship coaching community. I no longer felt invisible or like an outsider looking in. To this day, I invest heavily in my stepfamily and professional educations, knowing that stepmoms around the world *struggle* to find their own identities and to fit within a mold that's either ill-conceived (a la The Evil Stepmom) or ill-fitting (The Mom vs. A Mom). Like I once had, they inadvertently sabotage their relationships by not knowing how to identify their concerns and empathize with others.

When we don't feel we belong, we wither away. We become invisible. We lose our voices, as well as our sense of independence and our individual identities. I want to stop this insanity by creating a sisterhood of women. Women who work to ensure the good of their stepfamilies free of competition, jealousy and bitterness. Women with care, love and peace in their hearts who can benefit from a more harmonious home life. Stepfamilies hurl mountains of hurt our way. Stepkids say they hate us. Exes shun us. Our partners sometimes tire of tedious conversation.

Yet, we never give up—do we? By now, you may have read *A Stepmom's Book of Boundaries* cover to cover. You and your partner may even have begun using some of the worksheets included in the Appendix, finally getting on the same page when it comes to: boundaries, House Rules and everything else they entail. So, what next? As with any work of this kind, there's no way I can condense years of knowledge into one single book. Instead, I encourage you to view this title as a stepping stone that gets you, your partner and your stepfamily closer to knowing how and where to draw the line for increased peace of mind and more positive outcomes.

Still, I'd love to continue this conversation with you. You're welcome and encouraged to follow me on Facebook, Twitter, Instagram and LinkedIn. Use the hashtag #StepmomCoach to highlight any questions or personal stories you'd like to share with me. Visit me online at TheStepmomCoach.com, where you'll find additional resources and information about setting and enforcing healthy boundaries. Be on the lookout for companion products like a standalone workbook and upcoming e-courses related to *A Stepmom's Book of Boundaries*. Remember, too, that boundaries are a challenge for all stepfamilies. Yes, all of them!

It's difficult to know when to step in and when to back off. There is no one-size-fits-all solution to doing it right, when it comes to addressing your stepfamily's unique dynamics and specific challenges. If you're looking for individualized help with your particular situation, contact me directly. I'd be honored to help you create a stronger, healthier stepfamily—taking it one, deliberate step forward at a time!

Warmly,
Claudette

Claudette Chenevert
The Stepmom Coach
Call/text: (703) 915-2470
Claudette@StepmomCoach.com

P.S. – Looking for even more advice? Sign up to receive my free e-newsletter for stepmoms at StepmomCoach.com.

APPENDIX

Arriving at Must-Have House Rules (see Chapter 11: Problem Areas, House Rules & Consequences)

When it comes to weak or nonexistent boundaries, you and your partner now know which problem areas trouble you—so, it's time to take action! This exercise helps you stretch a little further, setting Stepfamily House Rules which are easier to enforce by increasing everyone's sense of ownership, accountability and achievement. You'll see two sets of questions. Discuss the first set among yourselves. Discuss the second set with the help of your older (step-)children, encouraging and allowing them to be involved in the process.

What does stepfamily life look like to you—the (step-)parents?

1. Will anyone share a bedroom and/or bathroom?
2. If so, how are space/time divided? Who gets priority?
3. Are friends allowed in kids' bedrooms? For how long?
4. Are TVs, computers and games okay in kids' bedrooms?
5. What content is okay? What time will they be powered off?
6. If food is allowed in the kids' bedrooms, is anything off-limits?
7. Will garbage be disposed of in kitchen or in bedroom trash cans?
8. If you'll spend Stepfamily Time together: How often? Doing what?
9. Are chores to be divided up? If so, who will be assigned which tasks?
10. Will chores rotate or stay the same? Do kids get their choice of chores?
11. Who decides when a chore is done? Is completion tied to an allowance?
12. Are meals to be eaten together at a set time or when everyone is hungry?
13. If a stepfamily member misses a meal, are there consequences tied to that?
14. Will the same person prepare all meals or will everyone take turns cooking?
15. Will those who don't cook then have to set/clear the table and/or wash dishes?

16. Who'll decide what's kept in the fridge? Who'll shop/buy food for the family?
17. When and where will homework be completed? Will it be checked? By whom?
18. Will all laundry be done together? If not, how will it be handled? Who does what?
19. Will you have pets? If so, what kind? Who'll then care for them, buy pet food, etc.?
20. Will everyone adhere to the same faith and/or need to go to church? If so, which one(s)?

The next set of questions is primarily aimed at the older kids in your home. As you consider them, think: If this teen or young adult weren't under our roof, how would we want them to handle these situations? Offer guidance that can benefit them in real-world situations, teaching them the lasting value of teamwork, responsibility and self-reliance.

Kids, what does stepfamily life look like to you?

1. Who sets curfew time?
2. What curfew hour seems fair?
3. What effect will missing curfew have?
4. If you run late, how will you handle this?
5. Who'll pay for car expenses: gas, repairs, etc.?
6. Who'll pay for traffic tickets and any related costs?
7. What effect will a DUI/DWI have? Who pays for that?
8. While in school, will you have a P/T job? Why/Why not?
9. Who'll pay for special outings/activities you're involved in?
10. Are sleepovers okay? And what about opposite-sex sleepovers?
11. What happens if you "borrow" someone else's stuff without asking?
12. Is smoking/drinking alcohol at home okay? What will happen if you do?
13. If you've moved back home for now, do you plan to work and how often?
14. If you've moved back home for now, when do you plan to move back out?
15. If you've moved back home for now, will you help pay bills? Why/Why not?

NOTE: While these questions are intentionally aimed at the teen and young adult members of your stepfamily, you and your partner must remain actively involved in setting behavioral guidelines, House Rules and consequences for everyone. That holds true for anything which affects the people you share your home with.

Stepfamily House Rule Conversation Starters (*see* Chapter 12: Setting Rules & Boundaries—Together!)

As you begin setting Stepfamily House Rules and attaching consequences to behaviors which violate them, these conversation starters give you something to go by. Add some of your own, addressing your own unique situation!

Manners

- Punctuality and tardiness
- "Please," "Thank you," etc.
- Greeting/acknowledging each other
- Answering doors or phones and taking messages
- Respecting Stepfamily Time, Couple's Time and Alone Time
- _____
- _____

Hygiene

- Washing hands before meals
- Washing hands after using the bathroom
- Flushing the toilet and restocking toilet paper
- _____
- _____

Behaviors

- Showing respect for others
- Screaming, cussing or name calling
- Handling disagreements or arguments
- Taking turns when talking and listening
- _____
- _____

Chores

- Mealtime chores
- Laundry procedures
- Trash, yardwork, pet care, etc.
- Will rewards/allowances depend on completion?
- _____
- _____

Common Spaces

- Phone and computer use
- Bathroom schedules, if sharing
- Opening/closing doors (no slamming)
- Retrieval and placement of incoming mail
- _____
- _____

Private Spaces

- Do doors remain open or closed?
- Are they kept clean or allowed to be messy?
- Are adults permitted to enter kids' spaces at will or not?
- Are TVs, computers or cell phones allowed in kids' rooms?
- If bedrooms are shared by children, how is space divvied up?
- _____
- _____

Personal Belongings

- How are they defined?
- Where are they to be kept?
- Are they allowed to move between homes or not?
- Can others borrow them? If so, how does that happen?
- _____
- _____

Time Spent with Friends

- Curfews/time limits
- Requesting sleepovers
- Taking turns going there/coming here
- When to ask permission and who to ask
- _____
- _____

Clothing, Gifts & Toys

- Paying for clothing purchases
- Weekly, monthly or annual budgets
- Whether they can move between homes or not
- Which gifts and/or toys must remain in the home
- _____
- _____

Education & Other Expenses

- Which schools will they go to?
- Who will pay for school tuition/fees?
- Will the kids' grades affect participation?
- Budgeting/paying for sports and activity expenses
- _____
- _____

Our Boundaries, Defined (*see* Chapter 14: What Stepfamily Boundaries Won't Do for You)

Use this worksheet—and the knowledge you've gained by reading *The Stepmom's Book of Boundaries*—to embark on a path that's paved with healthier boundaries, enforceable House Rules and a stepfamily experience that rewards your stepfamily with its own version of the white-picket-fence dream. Complete it as a couple or photocopy it and complete it individually. Just be sure to come together and arrive at a combined plan that works for both of you!

Getting Clear About Boundaries

My/our definition of a boundary is:

_____
_____
_____
_____
_____
_____

(3) boundaries our stepfamily has in place now:

✓ _____
✓ _____
✓ _____

(3) *new* boundaries we could set for our stepfamily:

O _____
O _____
O _____

When it comes to enforcing boundaries and House Rules, in our home ...

It's my responsibility to:

_____

It's my partner's responsibility to:

_____

Boundaries, Behaviors & Consequences

(3) ways *healthier* stepfamily boundaries will benefit us:

- o _____
- o _____
- o _____

(3) ways unhealthy or missing stepfamily boundaries hurt us:

- o _____
- o _____
- o _____

In the past, a lack of boundaries has caused:

_____
_____
_____
_____

Going forward, establishing boundaries will help us:

_____
_____
_____
_____

Modeling Appropriate Behaviors

(3) ways I could model appropriate behavior:

- o _____
- o _____
- o _____

(3) ways my partner could model appropriate behavior:

- o _____
- o _____
- o _____

It's important to *show* children how to behave versus *tell* them how to behave.

In my/our view, that's because:

_____

_____

_____

_____

(3) values/beliefs we share, as partners:

✓ _____

✓ _____

✓ _____

(3) related boundaries we can set *for* our stepfamily:

O _____

O _____

O _____

(3) values/beliefs we share, as a stepfamily:

✓ _____

✓ _____

✓ _____

(3) related boundaries we can set *as* a stepfamily:

O _____

O _____

O _____

Communicating Your Boundaries

Refer back to chapters on setting realistic boundaries and communicating them clearly. Then, use this checklist to make sure you've covered all the bases. Once you and your partner are in agreement, call a Stepfamily Meeting. Welcome the children's input on boundaries and House Rules, yet remember to guide them to the sorts of behaviors you believe will ensure everyone's safety, security, privacy and well-being.

- ☐ Prioritize your stepfamily's current needs.
- ☐ Identify any boundaries which may be lacking.
- ☐ Develop a combined list of related House Rules.
- ☐ Decide which are negotiable and non-negotiable.
- ☐ Clearly lay out any/all associated consequences.
- ☐ Share the list openly in a Stepfamily Meeting.
- ☐ Give each child a chance to offer feedback.
- ☐ Arrive at all final decisions in private.
- ☐ Post your House Rules prominently.

Feedback received during the meeting:

_____
_____
_____
_____
_____
_____

Notes to Self/Other:

_____
_____
_____
_____
_____
_____

ABOUT CLAUDETTE

C laudette began her own stepmom journey in 1990, when she met the man who'd rock her world forever. Though already a mom, she had no idea that adjusting to stepfamily life would turn that world upside down. Lulled by images of "The Sound of Music" and "The Brady Bunch," she thought it was simple: You get married, bring the kids home and sing a song in perfect harmony. Losing all sense of identity and control, she found herself straddling biological fault lines along which boundaries seemed nonexistent and she was no longer her husband's No. 1.

Hitting rock bottom, she sought therapy. It was there she found a solution. At age 36, this former hairdresser—with a knack for helping others recognize and be inspired by their own beauty within—went back to school. Upon graduating with honors, she launched her career as a Stepfamily & Relationship Coach. Claudette is now a Master Certified Stepfamily Foundation Coach who specializes in human behavior, communication and relationship dynamics. She's also a member of the Int'l. Coach Federation and the Int'l. Positive Psychology Association.

Claudette has one son, two stepdaughters and seven grandchildren. She and her husband, Bernard, travel between the U.S. and Canada by RV. She shares her expertise with a worldwide audience of stepmoms and stepcouples as both The Stepmom Coach and a *StepMom Magazine* contributor. Visit her anytime at StepmomCoach.com.

ACKNOWLEDGEMENTS

I enjoy writing most when it's for no other reason than to let my thoughts wander and to capture whatever comes to mind. Writing a book is a totally different endeavor; so much planning and thought go into pulling it all together. Just like raising kids and having a family takes a village, many people have (directly or indirectly) contributed to making *The Stepmom's Book of Boundaries* a reality. I've done my best to acknowledge most of them below, though there are others who have helped in various ways.

None of my work would be possible without the support and encouragement of my husband. Bernard, thank you for always making sure I'm fed and for the endless supply of coffee. Your patience can exceed mine and I'm grateful for that. You also provide the best support by picking up the slack in our home and by telling it like it is when I share a piece of writing with you. I thank my stepdaughters and my son—Julie, Stephanie and Sebastien—for helping us define and then test the boundaries we set in our shared home. Each of you continues to help clarify what's acceptable in our lives and what's not. I know you're busy establishing boundaries for your own children now and am grateful for the grandkids you've given us: Taylor, Paul, Rebecca, Mason, Lucas, Logan and Jackson.

Josy Labbe, I am blessed to have a best friend in you. You've stood by me through some of my most difficult and challenging times. Our friendship has taught me that firm, clear boundaries help each of us thrive and that we all deserve to be treated respectfully and lovingly. Sharona E.S., thank you for engaging me in long, philosophical discussions; the kind which help us walk away more enlightened about life's challenges, our worldviews and ourselves. In a similar vein, decades of study and research have helped me understand my own situation and have ensured that Bernard and I didn't wind up a stepfamily statistic. I have several people to thank for that.

Patricia L. Papernow, EdD, thank you for discussing this book with me, for sharing a number of professional insights and for providing invaluable feedback. Jeannette Lofas, PhD, thank you for opening doors to understanding with your emphasis on the distinct needs of stepfamilies and through your work with The Stepfamily Foundation. John M. Gottman, PhD, your research and training programs have given me hope, expanded my understanding of healthy relationships and taught me to be more empathic and curious when it comes to my husband and our kids.

Brené Brown, PhD, your work on shame and vulnerability continues to teach us all that setting boundaries isn't the same as setting up walls of protection. It also reinforces the fact that boundaries make it safer to be ourselves and to open up to one another. Margie Warrell, I have you to thank for writing *Find Your Courage* and *Brave*. Both have served as reminders of why I began writing this book in the first place: To help stepmoms worldwide feel more empowered. And Michelle Weiner-Davis, through your book *Divorce Busting*, you taught me that there were alternatives to handling relationship stress and that the first step itself was to set healthy boundaries.

A very special thanks to Brenda Ockun, founder and publisher of *StepMom Magazine*. You gave me the chance to share my training and expertise with more stepmoms than I ever thought possible. Your mentoring and support, from my earliest days as a contributor to your groundbreaking publication, have encouraged me to write the book which has been stirring inside of me. And, while writing comes naturally to me, editing and proofreading aren't my strengths. So, thanks for introducing me to the woman who'd eventually edit *The Stepmom's Book of Boundaries.* It would be incomplete without the help of Christine G. Adamo at WriteReviseEdit.com (dba "A-ha!" Creative).

Christine, you taught me that it's one thing to write content and another to compile everything needed to deliver lasting value in book form. Your guidance helped me organize my thoughts. Your editing enhanced the flow of my ideas and my early drafts. Your contributions—including your knowledge, expertise and amazing cover design skills—resulted in a cohesive product I'm thrilled to share with the world. I'm proud to have you on my team and to call you my friend. Colleen Simons, I know that you also spent many hours combing through each chapter to help ensure that no known errors slipped past us and that every sentence made sense. For that, I am grateful.

Finally? I must give special thanks to every stepmom who has shared her individual story with me over the years. Working with you to improve your stepfamily relationships is a privilege and an honor. Learning more about your unique situation continues to inspire and motivate me. Hearing from you by email or by phone brightens my day, especially when you tell me that working with me—in my role as The Stepmom Coach—has had a positive impact on you and your stepfamily. You have trusted me enough to share your entire journey with me, including your anger, sadness, hope, joy, frustration, despair, success, etc.

While I will not name you publicly, you know who you are. Thank you!

Made in the USA
Middletown, DE
24 March 2019